PRAISE FOR REISSMAN AND GURA'S
TEACHING WITH AUTHOR WEB SITES, K–8

"As a folklorist, writer, and teacher of writing, I know firsthand how interactive author web sites make it possible for students to talk, meet, and exchange ideas with extraordinary writers. With the click of a mouse, a writer enters into a student's universe in a new way—and literature itself moves closer to home. Reissman, a transformative teacher, and Gura, one of New York City's strongest proponents of technology and education, have devised a brilliant strategy for utilizing the World Wide Web in the service of literacy. This book offers a wide range of opportunities for teachers and students to use these free resources to foster literacy and learning in the classroom."

—Steve Zeitlin

Director, City Lore

"As a manager of the NY Daily News eEdition, I believe teachers need to tap author sites and eEditions to foster engaged literacy. This book, with its strategies for connecting teachers with online author sites, helps make literature come alive for students."

—Lauren Gurnee

NIE Assistant Manager, Educational Programs, The New York Daily News

"A ready-to-go resource for teachers of 21st-century literacy. While many see the need for digital-age curriculum, just what to do and how to do it often remain a mystery. Road maps like this one that blaze a clear path for bringing The New Learning into our nation's classrooms are exactly what's needed just now!"

—Marina Leight

Editor in Chief, Converge Magazine

"A fantastic tool for educators to utilize in their classroom, shortening the distance between the educator and the author and expanding the horizons of the classroom into the World Wide Web. Whether it be listening to a podcast, reading a biographical essay, or simply viewing family pictures, the text-to-author connection is easily facilitated using this practical and handy implement."

—Chaia Frishman

In-House Literacy Developer, Yeshiva Darchei Torah

"A gift to the social studies educator that provides a teacher-ready means to integrate technology, literacy, and citizenship learning into primary, elementary, and middle school classrooms. During this period of high-stakes testing when social studies content is often ignored for English language arts and mathematics test focus, this work by two talented and veteran educators shows how author Web studies can immediately connect students to social studies content and civic goals while they become ongoing readers and writers."

—David Keller Trevaskis

Executive Director, LEAP-Kids,
President, Pennsylvania Council for the Social Studies

"This valuable tool brings a new dimension to the teaching of reading and literacy, giving teachers a chance to further engage their students. It gives teachers and students the opportunity to analyze, discuss, and integrate the personal element into the curriculum across subject areas, with very explicit and detailed instruction."

—Shifra Hanon

Language Arts Teacher and Enrichment Supervisor,

Yeshiva of Flatbush High School, Brooklyn, NY

"A reference such as this has been needed for some time. Educators and parents alike will benefit from this book, which will make 21st-century education a 'mission: possible.'"

—Daniel Stein

Professor, Touro College

"Mark and Rose provide a myriad of strategies for using author sites, blogs, and other multimedia resources to connect students with authors whose works they study in class or read on their own. The book is a terrific convergence of technology and literacy that will result in students becoming lifelong pursuers of literacy engagement."

—Bernard Percy

Producer/Educator, Author of The Power of Creative Writing

"As the head of NYC Mind Lab Thinking Skills Training Centers and Futurekids Literacy Technology Centers, I can readily see that integrating use of author Web sites into ongoing literacy and technology student-centered projects will reciprocally enhance lifelong multimedia and print literacy. It is so good to see the work of these two veteran classroom educators and researchers available to teachers K–8."

—Stephane Ifrah

President & CEO, FUTUREKIDS and Mind Lab, NY

"Reissman and Gura provide educators a very realistic approach for seamlessly weaving technology and instruction. Their approach is practical, while keeping in sight what should be our ultimate goal as educators: cultivating lifelong learners, not just short-term test-takers. Younger students' curiosity will be piqued through the use of technology, middle school students are motivated, and literacy becomes more meaningful for reluctant readers and writers."

—Veronica Cordero-Turner

Educator, Mt. Vernon City School District, NY

TEACHING
With **Author Web Sites**
K-8

Rose Cherie Reissman
Mark Gura

CORWIN
A SAGE Company

For information:

Corwin
A SAGE Company
2455 Teller Road
Thousand Oaks, California 91320
(800) 233-9936
Fax: (800) 417-2466
www.corwinpress.com

SAGE Ltd.
1 Oliver's Yard
55 City Road
London EC1Y 1SP
United Kingdom

SAGE India Pvt. Ltd.
B 1/I 1 Mohan Cooperative
    Industrial Area
Mathura Road, New Delhi 110 044
India

SAGE Asia-Pacific Pte. Ltd.
33 Pekin Street #02-01
Far East Square
Singapore 048763

Printed in the United States of America

Library of Congress Cataloging-in-Publication Data

Reissman, Rose.
Teaching with author Web sites, K-8 / Rose Cherie Reissman, Mark Gura.
    p. cm.
Includes bibliographical references and index.
ISBN 978-1-4129-7386-1 (pbk. : alk. paper)

    1. Education, Elementary—United States—Computer network resources. 2. Language arts (Elementary)—United States—Computer network resources 3. Internet in education—United States. 4. Authors—Directories. 5. Web sites for children—Directories. I. Gura, Mark. II. Title.

LB1044.87.R447 2010
372.6078'54678—dc22   2009028200

This book is printed on acid-free paper.

9   10   11   12   13   10   9   8   7   6   5   4   3   2   1

Acquisitions Editor:	Carol Chambers Collins
Editorial Assistant:	Brett Ory
Production Editor:	Amy Schroller
Copy Editor:	Sarah J. Duffy
Typesetter:	C&M Digitals (P) Ltd.
Proofreader:	Charlotte J. Waisner
Indexer:	Sheila Bodell
Cover Designer:	Michael Dubowe

Contents

Additional resources related to

Teaching With Author Web Sites, K-8 can be found at
http://sites.google.com/site/teachingwithauthorwebsites
and
http://teachingwithauthorwebsites.blogspot.com/

Acknowledgments

From Rose:

Sidonia Blank Reissman, my mother and literacy mentor, who taught me to love reading, writing, speaking, and presenting. Edward Stern, my first principal at Ditmas Education Complex, who told me I should develop curricula and train teachers. He set aside time for me to do that. These initial curricula efforts were the start of my career in educational leadership. Ditmas Educational Complex in Brooklyn, the public middle school in Brooklyn, where many of my article, book, and workshop ideas were field tested. The atmosphere of this warm literacy and professional community (Janie Bahnsen, Beatrice DeSapio, and Principal Barry Kevorkian) continues to nurture caring professionals and lifelong student learners.

PUBLISHER'S ACKNOWLEDGMENTS

Corwin gratefully acknowledges the contributions of the following reviewers:

Sue DeLay, Learning Support Teacher
Cedar Hills Elementary School
Oak Creek, WI

Michael Fisher, Coordinator
CSLO/Model Schools
Erie 1 Board of Cooperative Educational Services Campus
Buffalo, NY

Jill Gildea, Superintendent
Harrison School District #36
Wonder Lake, IL

Sheila M. Gragg, Technology Integration Coach/Professional Development Specialist
Ashbury College
Ottawa, Ontario, Canada

Joan Irwin, Professional Development Consultant
Newark, DE

Charity Jennings, Full-Time Faculty, Education
University of Phoenix
Seoul, South Korea

Michelle Strom, National Board Certified Teacher
Department of Defense Education Activity
Seoul, South Korea

About the Authors

Rose Cherie Reissman continues to work with students in classrooms across the country, teaching literacy, project-based learning, oral law history, law-related education, and museums in schools. Her classroom field testing of original strategies and projects has resulted in her publishing an ongoing series of articles, books, and curricula. She is president of the New York City Association of Teachers of English and a consultant for the *Daily News*. Dr. Reissman continues to teach graduate education courses and seminars across the country.

Mark Gura has been an educator for over thirty-five years. He is the former director of the Office of Instructional Technology of the New York City Department of Education, a professional development organization he developed after serving as a classroom teacher for eighteen years and a staff developer for five. He currently teaches graduate education courses for Fordham University and Touro College. Mr. Gura has written extensively about the use of technology across the curriculum, publishing numerous articles and books on the subject. He also cohosts The Teachers Podcast, a popular talk show about the use of technology for literacy instruction that has been downloaded over five million times. He blogs at http://markgura.blogspot.com.

I dedicate this book to all those authors whose work fired my imagination when I was a child. In school or out, I needed more inspiration than the adults in my world could give me face-to-face. And, of course, I dedicate it also to all those authors who now tap the Internet to stir the souls of similar kids growing up today. Through their web sites, their magic has far greater reach than that of the authors of my childhood who had print alone.

—Mark

Introduction

by Mark Gura

Rose first showed me her pioneering work in the use of author web sites a few years back when I was preparing to give a keynote presentation for the New York Reading Association. I was impressed with the huge potential this approach offered; it immediately clicked for me that this was the very thing for that vast majority of teachers out there who would like to find an easy way to bring technology into their classrooms. Using author web sites encourages the use of technology without the usual disincentives: the need for extensive professional development; the need for a significant influx of hardware, software, and peripheral devices; and most off-putting, the need to take a major detour from the familiar curriculum that they use with confidence. Using author sites eliminates all that while allowing a new and exciting dimension to be brought into the classroom. I could see these advantages instantly, and apparently so did my "non-techie" audience.

A few years back, before retirement, I was the director of The Office of Instructional Technology for the New York City Department of Education. The office served the city's eighty thousand teachers, who in turn taught 1.1 million students. My responsibility was to provide guidance, resources, instructional support, and professional development in the integration of technology across the curriculum. Because of the scope of this mandate, we learned to bypass all resources and practices that didn't resonate strongly with teachers. We avoided resources that required a significant outlay of funds and those that took time to set up. Those that required frequent maintenance were avoided, too. Instead, we turned our attention solely to practices that teachers could adopt within the limiting parameters of their jobs and that offered them real advantages in teaching and learning.

MINIMAL EQUIPMENT AND TECH SKILLS REQUIRED

Author web sites, which are *free,* are a perfect low-risk sandbox in which to play, try things out, learn, and adopt. Teachers who have access to a working computer with a connection to the Internet already have pretty much all they need to use them. Sure, some of these sites offer media items that may require the download of a plug-in or player (nothing hard to accomplish, just read and follow simple directions), but author sites are generally created by sophisticated webmasters who see their mission as providing clients with a resource that will run on almost anything. Thus, the sites are designed so that even if every item isn't viewed or heard at optimum capacity, they are still displayed at a level that will support their appreciation. Consequently, if a classroom computer runs a relatively up-to-date browser, not necessarily the most recent one, and is supported by a connection that approaches broadband, the overwhelming majority of author web sites will deliver their magic just fine.

Assuming that a teacher has some very basic computer and technology skills—like turning the computer on, manipulating a mouse, and opening and closing files—then there are very few things to learn in order to make author web sites a centerpiece of instruction. After launching a browser and finding and accessing an author's web site, the rest of the experience requires simply

1. Reading the directions on the web site (simple commands like "click here," "back," and "next," generally accompanied by arrows or other visual cues)

2. Following those directions

3. Left-clicking a mouse

Really, that's about it! Of course there are always a few other things that can be done. Author sites can be bookmarked, for instance, and their URLs can be e-mailed to students, parents, or colleagues. But generally, these tasks can also be accomplished with the simplest of commands, developed with the non–technically inclined in mind. These web sites are truly part of the new user-friendly digital literacy landscape.

Consequently, whatever professional development is offered relating to the use of author web sites has much less to do with the acquisition of technology skills than it does with using the sites' instructional resources. Staff development in the use of author web sites provides a wonderful bonus opportunity to discuss core instructional ideas that have a direct impact on literacy instruction, for example, the value and methodology of author study, the relationship between self-directed reading and writing, and the use of media.

IT'S SAFE

One of the common "yeah, buts" one hears about the use of the web as an instructional resource has to do with the fear that somehow web sites will put youngsters in jeopardy. And in fact, there are web sites with very unwholesome content that we do want to prevent youngsters from visiting. Author web sites, however, are generally resources that educators can use with confidence. These sites are authorized by and maintained for professional authors who fully understand the responsibility of keeping them appropriate for their young audience. Furthermore, a preferred manner of using these sites in the classroom is during whole-group instruction, in which the web destination the class visits is controlled by the teacher, who then moderates the students' experience of exploring it with an eye toward appropriateness and quality.

INSTRUCTION AND CLASSROOM MANAGEMENT

When it first became possible to bring the magic of computer technology into the classroom, many eager educators adopted the one-to-one environment—that is, one laptop for every student—as the ideal, exclusively relevant deployment model. Now that the dust is clearing on the classroom tech revolution and we've had time to reflect on how it has played out, it is becoming clear that one-to-one, as valuable as it may be in some situations, is just one model among several. In fact, its exclusive deployment throws off the balance of many teaching and learning factors. Think of it this way: in the course of a balanced educational experience, a classroom will have youngsters working independently at times, in small groups at others, and at other times still as a unified whole group. The class will toggle back and forth between modalities as the needs of learners shift.

The whole-group mode of instruction is a uniquely valuable approach to classroom technology use. Think about a scenario in which the teacher projects a large image for the whole class to work from, allowing students to view and participate as a group in web site navigation decisions. This approach, in which the whole class is able to view the same screen, is far more economical and practical logistically than individual instruction, with the teacher attempting to monitor and scaffold every student's navigation of a site. Anyone who has had the privilege of observing a skilled literacy teacher doing a book walk with a group of elementary students will recognize the connection. The teacher holds up a big book for students to admire, a literary talisman that is examined and admired before the book is formally "read" from more traditionally scaled, individual copies. This is very similar to a whole-group activity in which the focus of attention is a single, large image of a web site. This approach to classroom technology use can support a range of tech-based activities across the grades, wherever an author's web site has items of high value to offer. It has applicability across the curriculum and at every grade level.

Another benefit of this approach, and one that will ensure that teachers see classroom technology use as easy and nonthreatening, is how it relates to classroom management. With the teacher at the mouse of the single display (likely an LCD projector, large-screen monitor, or interactive whiteboard), few of the distracting behaviors that can get in the way of the flow of a well-planned lesson are likely to creep in. With the teacher asking for suggestions (by the traditional raising of hands and sharing with the group) about where to navigate the group's attention on the web sites being used, or calling individuals up to the mouse to take their turn at control, in no way has the interactivity been compromised. It has simply been adapted to the shared-activity mode of instruction that is a tried-and-true portion of the overall school experience.

WHY THIS BOOK IS IMPORTANT

Even though we are into the third decade of the field of instructional technology, technology integration remains a largely unfulfilled ideal in many schools. With the advent of reasonably priced and easily maintained personal computers, ever increasing access to broadband Internet service, and an exploding body of highly valuable web-based content, technology use across the curriculum really should have become the norm by now. Technologies that have positively transformed all realms of intellectual activity outside of education still remain something of an unattainable holy grail inside our classrooms.

All who weigh in on the subject—informed practitioner, policy maker, or plain old concerned citizen—agree that the time for pointing to pockets of success or examples of integration models is long past. So much work has been done in this field; it can no longer be said that we are still trying to figure out how to adapt technology for education. Search the web! The evidence and knowledge is there and in such quantities as to quell any doubts or questions.

Teachers from colleges of education to K–12 classrooms have called for the inclusion of technology as an important part of teaching and learning in the 21st century. A glance at the web sites of important professional organizations such as the National Council of Teachers of English, the International Reading Association, and the National Council of Teachers of Mathematics show a solidarity of interest among leading educators in improving students' proficiency in the new literacies of information and communication technology.

We understand that the use of technology will make the school experience more relevant for youngsters growing up in the current intellectual environment, fostering greater engagement and motivation, and likely resulting in improved attendance and graduation rates. The question is: What's needed to nudge this snowball over the rim of the mountain? What push will set it in motion so that the natural and inevitable law of gravity can take over?

Rather than set up pilot programs with specially trained teachers—the "classroom of the future" approach that has so often been taken and has produced so very little in the way of systemic change—a different tack will likely produce the effect we've sought for so long. What's needed is to develop a critical mass of technology-using teachers—teachers who make technology part and parcel of what they do as naturally as they might distribute a set of books to their class, direct their students to read a passage, and then conduct a whole-group discussion to clarify what's been read. Once this critical mass of non-techie teachers who are comfortably using technology has become a reality, the rest of the technology integration puzzle will likely fall into place. Classroom technology use will go from being extraordinary to ordinary.

To achieve this critical mass, what's needed are rock solid, perennial, "must do, tried and true" classroom activities, practices that require an amount of professional development and preparation that the vast rank-and-file mass of teachers find reasonable and doable as part of their professional lives. These must be practices with threshold levels of technology that are accessible and not intimidating.

Author study is, in my mind, one of those "killer app" key entry point practices poised and ready to make broad-based technology integration a reality. Author web sites are a perfect tech resource; they are hyper user-friendly, free, and ubiquitous. They fit into the existing curriculum easily. They enrich the experience of students and teachers tremendously. They are good to go tomorrow or, better yet, today! This is a tech application that appeals to all stakeholders: teachers, students, parents, and administrators.

Furthermore, author web sites, with their embedded media items bring the new life of books into classrooms that otherwise would present an antiquated print-only understanding of them. The *way* of books, and the world around them, has changed. While the centerpiece of their existence remains a hard-copy presence, the orbit surrounding books, particularly the connection to authors, is very much a web-based experience. Author sites illustrate this in important ways that are easy to grasp.

For all these reasons and more, digital author study—facilitated through the use of author web sites—is likely to be adopted by content area leaders who will sooner or later come to realize that it offers easy-to-achieve, innovation-driven change. It's a change that profoundly improves the classrooms they are responsible for supporting and holding accountable for success. This is important because it is the leaders and supervisors of core content area instruction that have the power and authority to make change happen in our schools when it comes to the adoption of technology. It will never be easy for instructional technologists to lobby for deep changes in the content area classrooms of our schools. However, instructional leaders in the areas of English language arts, science, math, social studies, and others, in partnership with supportive instructional technologists, can make such changes happen easily and quickly. Author web sites are a ready-to-go resource that can be tapped for this immediately.

WHO GETS TURNED ON TO LITERACY BY AUTHOR WEB SITES?

Not only teachers, but above all students will love using author web sites for key literacy activities. These sites are more than simply motivating and engaging; they are enticing. Students who haven't been able to demonstrate comprehension skills and appropriate literacy responses—couldn't answer rote questions in a basal textbook about plot, sequencing, style, or theme when only permitted to use print materials—suddenly light up with wonderful "got it" smiles when visiting author sites. With focused technology use, students properly guided by tech-savvy teachers are supported to deal successfully with the very same literacy components that may have eluded them continually in spoken text-only lessons.

Students who've never responded to their teacher's writing prompts, even though they may have been masterfully modeled with the teacher's personal writing, begin to eagerly write when the prompts come from an author they encounter online. Highly popular authors such as T. A. Barron, Jean Craighead George, or Judy Blume offer many such opportunities through their web sites.

Students who never contribute to classroom discussion because of self-consciousness about talking in front of others, whether due to low English language proficiency or just plain shyness, are happily productive contributors when they can participate in an online discussion about an author's work. These same students' faces often light up when they see their comments displayed on the discussion board of, for example, author Gregory Maguire's web site—just one of many ways that authors' sites successfully enfranchise and enroll students in the circle of readers and writers.

English Language Learners who may only hear English spoken in the classroom, not in their homes, become attentive and excited as they see pictures of authors at their age online in author site galleries. They can also follow video presentations online and access web sites of authors who write in their native language.

Once students enter these sites, they are presented with some of the potentially best content to be found. This book offers a starting point for educators interested in understanding and tapping that potential.

OVERVIEW OF THIS BOOK

In Chapter 1, the basic components of author sites are reviewed and their direct application to instruction is discussed. Chapter 2 focuses on the web site of Eric Carle, a favorite classroom author, and gives a detailed understanding of how the components of author sites fit well within required standards-based curriculum. Chapter 3 offers a walk through the web site of T. A. Barron, who provides valuable literacy and social studies content. Chapter 4 presents an interview with author Judy Blume, in which she explains why and how she uses her web site to make her writings and social concerns come alive for students, teachers, and parents. Chapter 5 focuses on author/illustrator sites where pictures drive the narrative, offering teachers many ways to use spatial entry points to promote literacy. Finally, Chapter 6 demonstrates how all teachers and their students can use Web 2.0 to create their own web sites with their responses to an author study.

Throughout the chapters, activities related to content are included both in the text and in highlighted features. Further activities are provided in companion web sites (http://teaching withauthorwebsites.blogspot.com, http://sites.google.com/site/teachingwithauthorwebsites). At the end of each chapter is an annotated list of additional author sites and web resources to explore. The appendix details how author study that uses online resources can be directly connected to standards in technology, to English language arts, and across the curriculum.

1

Welcome to the World of Authors and Readers Online

Welcome to the world of author web sites! Like Pam Muñoz Ryan's site (see Figure 1.1), this book is for "educators, the most dedicated readers of all, who are looking for information that might enhance the reading experience of their students." In this book we describe how to make use of these rich web resources in your classroom, not only as a portal and extension to that time-honored language arts activity, author study, but across the curriculum. As educators who have been working with teachers for

Figure 1.1 Screenshot from Pam Muñoz Ryan's web site

decades with this approach to technology-supported literacy learning, we know it will become a welcome part of your practice and help you pass the love of books to students—particularly those grappling with making reading part of their lives.

True, some of the practice and pedagogy presented here could in fact be done with just books, texts, and print materials without the use of technology. But using the web sites as indicated throughout these pages will make the experience so much richer. The classroom will become a place of infinite intellectual excitement and satisfaction as students acquire required literacy skills along with a lifelong passion for literature, authors, and reading as a lifestyle.

For some students, the use of technology is itself the hook. We have found a strikingly high level of student engagement when the use of author web sites is introduced. So-called reluctant readers or resistant readers rush to the computer. Once there, they sit mesmerized in front of their monitors as they are put in touch with authors who may have left them cold when print books were their sole calling cards. Through the authors' web sites and the remarkable treasures they offer, the students' experience is positively transformed. Reading takes on the aspects of exploring, of using a variety of one's senses, and of playing. The authors' literary work, digitally enhanced, comes alive on the web and has the power to turn many students into emerging readers.

Every educator in the field of literacy, including librarians, literacy coaches, and reading specialists, knows the excitement and thrill students get from meeting a *real* author in their classroom, school library, or local bookstore. This is especially so when students have already read one or more works by the author and learned a bit of his or her life story. Their heightened anticipation and the thrill of meeting that author in person often turns them into lifelong readers—readers who continue to savor the author's work and who venture far beyond it, avidly consuming the works of others once they get the feel and pleasure of it.

VIRTUAL AUTHOR APPEARANCES

But how often does an author whose works you and your students are studying as part of your planned curriculum actually make a scheduled school, public library, or local book-store appearance? This most valuable experience may be available to classes once, or per-haps a few times a year if the school has unusually generous literacy funding. For those who teach and learn in rural or inner-city schools, the opportunity is even less likely to be available. Most students never get the benefit of direct interaction with the authors of the liter-ary works they study.

The author web site, however, allows you—as long as your school is wired and has Internet access—to bring a celebrity, curriculum-connected author right into your classroom and on your own schedule. Far more accessible than those rare in-person visits, a web visit makes author contact possible anytime it's desired and at any point during author study or reading and writing activities inspired by an author's work.

But can these web-based experiences really offer the richness of a real "live" author appearance? With proper understanding and preparation, the answer is yes. Just as students can be prompted and prepared for profitable classroom viewing of theatrical film or television presentations based on print books and related materials, so too can they be prepped to take advantage of authors' sites. If you take time to preview an author's efforts online, investing no more than 5–10 minutes, you can pick up little-known details about the author's life, interests, books, and pet causes—all of which can help you enrich the experience you offer to students.

A good site for your first visit is that of Pam Muñoz Ryan, a prolific, award-winning, bestselling author of books for young people, including *Esperanza Rising, Paint the Wind,* and *Nacho and Lolita.* Figure 1.1, at the beginning of the chapter, shows the landing page from her official web site (www.pammunozryan.com). Her web site is emblematic of how this new tool continues to change writing, reading, and learning for the better; notice in the screen shot in Figure 1.1 how she has incorporated information that students might need for an author study or book report. Like many author sites, Ryan's also includes a link to a video interview.

TRY THIS WITH YOUR CLASS

Activity 1.1 Welcome Screen Set-Up

Grades 3–8

1. Select an author whose works are familiar to students, or have students individually select a favorite author.

2. Before they check out the author's site (or one that the publisher provides), challenge students to create a welcome screen or landing page for their favorite author (like the one in Figure 1.1).

3. As background, discuss with students what type of opening screens various author sites have (e.g., a photo of the writer with pets or tools of writing or art, a graphic of a writer's most famous character).

4. Review a number of examples with students, and reflect on what you find.

5. Present one sample screen shot as a focus. Challenge students to explain why they think it was selected for this important introduction.

6. Have students work in teams or independently to write about, draw, and perhaps collage with downloaded or clipped-out images their own suggested first screens for their favorite authors' sites.

7. Make certain that each student or team can explain their selection of images, photos, and graphics plus text for the author site. If a particular type of music or digital special effect would be appropriate for an author, have students explain why they would use it for the site.

8. After students share their anticipated and desired first screens for favorite authors, have them examine the actual first screens of the author sites. Facilitate a class discussion and/or ask students to reflect in writing on the extent to which the actual welcome screen matched, differed, or bettered their designs.

9. As an extension, encourage students to submit these design ideas to some of the author sites for author or webmaster feedback.

10. As a further extension, if the school has the resources and you and the students have the technological skills, have them use web authoring software or Web 2.0 online resources (e.g., Blogger) to begin their own fan sites in the spirit of official author sites (see also Chapter 6).

A LOOK AT AUTHOR WEB SITES

Authors put up web sites for many reasons. These sites function as public relations and advertising campaign, bookstore, post office, and customer relations office all rolled into one. They are a one-stop-shopping point of contact between the author and potential readers, new and long-term readers, hardcore fans, and all sorts of people interested in them and their work.

Authors discovered long ago that readers are intensely interested not just in books, but in the people who write those books, particularly books that move them somehow. A web site is a perfect platform from which readers and visitors can obtain exactly the background information that the author wants to make available. Generally, telling their own story results in increased interest and, down the road, increased sales, appearances, and opportunities.

Web sites also help readers get in touch with authors. They facilitate correspondence, often through forms embedded in the web site or an e-mail link that encourages readers to write to them. By posting much of the basic background information ordinarily requested, the author can move past this and be freed up to answer more in-depth questions on a one-on-one basis. This is also a way for the author to glean feedback about books, doing market research for future writing efforts. Furthermore, some author web sites have guest books or message functions that allow readers and fans to leave comments that can be shared with other visitors, a way to share their enthusiasm for an author, to cast their vote in favor of an author's work, so to speak.

Teachers will find information and suggestions on how to use the author's works with students, lesson plans, and ancillary materials that can be used to enrich instructional activities. Students will find games, entertainment items, and advice on how to write—all related to the work of the author whose site they are visiting.

There are certainly many other types of web sites with information about authors; publishers' sites, fan sites, "webliographies," and others all have information about authors and their works. The official web site put up or sanctioned by an author is a very special one, however, and generally is lavished with the most personal and interesting material. On an authorized site, teachers and readers can be certain that the facts, ideas, design, and experiences there are approved by the actual author or someone who has received approval from the author or his or her estate. This book is primarily directed at the official sites that authors feel generally offer the best option for digital author study.

Features of Author Web Sites

Although author web sites sometimes have some unique features specific to the authors for which they are created, they have quite a few components in common.

Home Page or Landing Page

- Welcome message: may have accompanying music, animations, sound effects, and so on
- Site map: an overview of what's to be found on the site and where it's located
- Internal links to the various pages and sections of the site
- External links to other web sites selected by the author or web site manager
- Web site info: date last updated, name of webmaster, copyright and source of information, and so on

Informational Features

- Bio of the author (with photos of family, childhood, pets, interests, etc.): sometimes includes a timeline of the author's life milestones (see Figure 1.1a)
- Publications/catalogue: a list of all the works by the author; sometimes also called the "author's bookshelf"
- Upcoming: sometimes listed as "in press" or "what's next," books that the author is currently working on or that will be published within the next year
- Galleries: author biographical and appearance photos, sometimes including jacket cover art
- FAQs: frequently asked questions about the author's work along with the author's answers

Contact Features

- Guest book
- E-mail link

Writing Tips

- Writing tips: prompts for young writers or reflections on the inspirations for various works the author has produced; sometimes includes general advice and insight on how to write

Extras

- Stories or books other than those written by the author
- Special programs the author has established, like contests or awards for students
- Audio clips/video clips of the author doing readings of published works
- Information about the author's interests or activities other than writing
- Trivia/quizzes on book characters, plot happenings, and so on

Author News

- Newsletters
- Schedule of the author's personal appearances
- Articles or interviews featuring the author

BALANCING LITERACY FOR NEW MILLENIALS

Finding a Place and Time for Digital Author Studies

Author web site–enriched literacy experiences, or any technology-driven approach for teaching reading and writing for that matter, may seem beside the point currently as educators have been mandated to go down what seem to them to clearly be other paths. School districts are very focused on test scores, teacher accountability, and initiatives to intensify and deepen literacy learning in content areas other than English language arts. In this era of No Child Left Behind and public demand for accountability, school accreditation and teaching success are based on student scores on standardized assessments, and the relationship between this and the riches found on author sites may not be apparent.

Teachers have to make certain that students learn and use various types of writing formats for their required literacy responses, including these:

- Procedural accounts (how-to or step-by-step)
- Procedural narratives
- Research reports
- Informational brochures
- Functional documents
- Poetry
- Science observations
- Short and extended responses to mathematical problems with paragraphs detailing how the students solved a particular mathematics calculation or used reading skills to comprehend what operation was needed to solve a word problem

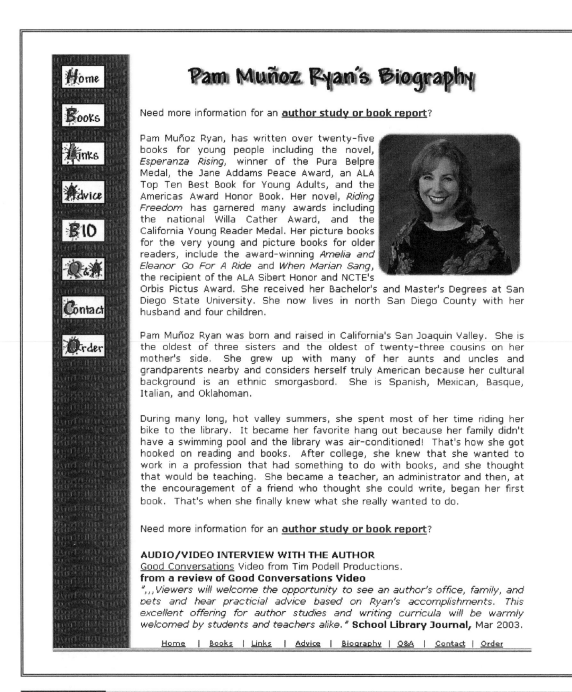

Figure 1.1a Screenshot of the bio page from Pam Munoz Ryan's web site

To add to this, many districts have adapted balanced literacy approaches for teaching reading and writing. These often require teachers to follow prescribed or scripted approaches such as the balanced literacy reading and writing workshop format for all lessons, with little margin for experimentation leftover.

Balanced Literacy: What and Why?

A popular approach to literacy instruction that has been highly influential over the past couple of decades is balanced literacy. It has become so pervasive that in order to explore

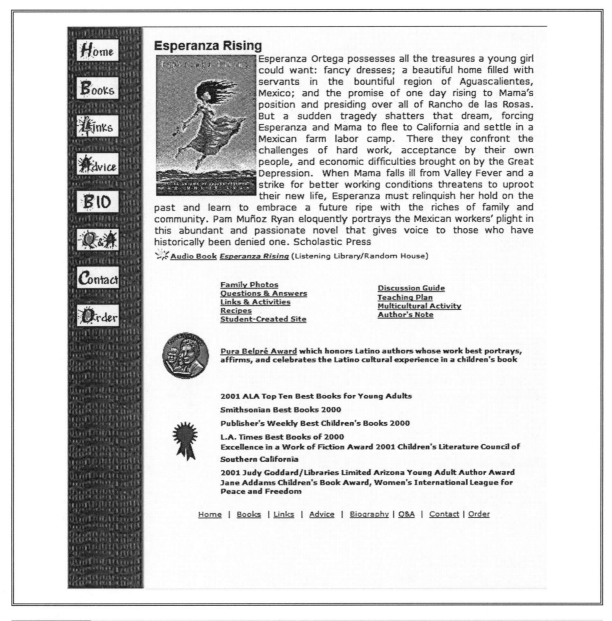

Figure 1.1b A page from Pam Muñoz Ryan's web site highlighting one of her popular works

how any new set of resources, and the practices involved in implementing them, can be adopted, one really ought to do so in light of compatibility with balanced literacy. However, like any widely adopted and adapted instructional philosophy that has been shaped by the work of a great many experts, a precise definition of the term is difficult. Nevertheless, teachers would do well to become informed about the following basic understandings about balanced literacy.

Balanced literacy is an attempt (successful in the judgment of many) to resolve the longstanding disagreement about how to effectively teach reading and writing—one school of thought holding that the teaching of basic skills is essential, the other that by teaching works of literature, teachers help students learn skills in context. In years gone by an "unbalanced" approach to reading instruction was taken either by stressing phonics and grammar or by implementing a whole-language approach with a focus on literature.

Balanced literacy holds that by maintaining a balance between the two approaches, an effective program is presented to students.

Some of the core beliefs of balanced literacy include the understanding that reading and writing should be seen and taught as complementary and that how students are taught is as important as what they are taught. Consequently, a balanced literacy instructional program is conceived as having definite pedagogical components that include the following:

- For reading
  - Read-aloud
  - Shared reading
  - Guided reading
  - Independent reading
  - Word work
- For writing
  - Modeled writing
  - Shared writing
  - Guided writing
  - Independent writing

A popular method of implementing balanced literacy is the reading and writing workshop model. In this approach, juggling the many components of balanced literacy, in terms of time allocation and structuring a proper sequence of instruction, is handled by what many consider a rigid set of organization frameworks. These often feature set scripts that prescribe what teachers will say in presenting materials and ideas as well as the amount of time to be spent engaged in the various activities.

It is particularly interesting for our discussion to note that Dorothy Strickland (1997), a noted authority on balanced literacy and a former president of the International Reading Association, includes in her widely published "Five Rules of Thumb for Maintaining Balance" the following statement: "Integrate print and electronic materials effectively. That way, your classroom will reflect the multimedia world in which students live" (p. 45).

Making Digital Author Studies
Part of the Balanced Literacy Approach

As we have emphasized, students like author web sites. These sites' power to engage assures their usefulness for teaching and learning. Using them will enrich mandated author studies, something students very likely have to do anyway as author studies have always been part of teaching reading and writing and are currently an important part of balanced literacy instruction.

It may appear, however, that scarcity of instructional time represents an impediment to making much use of author web sites. After all, while the balanced literacy approach does include an author study component, even providing lists of suggested authors, it doesn't call for an extensive allotment of time for web site explorations. The typical school day is often very structured, commonly featuring a basic balanced literacy lesson plan format that includes a minilesson of 10–15 minutes, small-group work for 15–20 minutes, and a final sharing activity that lasts 10 minutes or so. Author study facilitated through the effective use of author web sites as instructional resources can easily be made to fit within the literacy workshop model that so many school districts have adopted. This is true even though the daily instructional schedule may initially seem to be arranged as indicated otherwise.

Guest Star Read-Alouds

One key component of a workshop-style balanced literacy lesson is a minilesson at the beginning of a class's literacy session. This involves the teacher providing direct instruction to the whole class, usually using a read-aloud or write-aloud activity. What's called for here is that the students listen while a reader, usually the teacher, reads aloud from a printed text or does a modeled write-aloud from a printed text, which is then the catalyst for the small-group work segment that follows.

Although a read-aloud or a spoken write-aloud is absolutely necessary as part of the balanced literacy workshop approach, it doesn't matter who reads aloud or voices the write-aloud modeling exercise. What's important is that the individual doing it is a highly literate speaker capable of modeling reading, speaking, and writing in an expressive motivational manner that will inspire the small-group and independent work that follows the minilesson.

So, could the read aloud for a T. A. Barron (www.tabarron.com) book, say the adventure story *The Last Years of Merlin* or the nonfiction book *The Hero's Trail,* be read aloud by . . . T. A. Barron himself? Would you trust the author to know how to read his own work expressively? Might the author provide a write-aloud giving his tips as a published and celebrated writer, and echoing the many children's trade books he writes, to inspire students as they create their own works? That would be fabulous and even better than the teacher reading the same selections, even if the teacher's speaking voice is wonderfully expressive. If T. A. Barron were to actually do a read-aloud for students working on his adventure/fantasy series or his nonfiction collection of young heroes who make a difference (www.barronprize.com), students would be thrilled to hear the actual voice of the author!

T. A. Barron's web site offers digital recordings that visitors can listen to. In the Book Readings section of his site, for instance, there are recordings of Barron reading the introduction

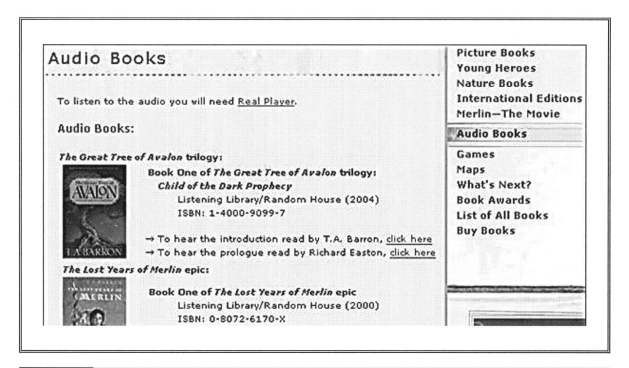

Figure 1.2   Screenshot from a page on T. A. Barron's web site offering audio clips of Barron reading selections from his popular books

or excerpts of quite a few of his books (see Figure 1.2). By clicking on these audio files, it is possible and easy to have T. A. Barron deliver a read-aloud.

Is there a more popular book with youngsters than *Charlie and the Chocolate Factory*? Perhaps *James and the Giant Peach* is a close second. As students work on these books by Roald Dahl, they can get to know him personally by listening to his answers to a number of questions about writing that have been asked of him and appear on his official web site (www.roalddahl.com). A common feature of a writing workshop lesson is the think-aloud in which the thinking behind literacy skills is modeled and reflected on. Using Dahl's web site, student writers could, after having heard his voice, continue to write an interview as he might respond to questions about his books and writing.

Another example connected to Pam Muñoz Ryan is that her presence can be summoned up in any classroom or home anytime through her recorded conversations. The video interview clip from her Good Conversations video (http://tinyurl.com/goodconversationryan) makes a great write-aloud. Although Ryan probably did not do that video to support the write-aloud component of the writing workshop, the practical advice and modeling of writing she discusses within the exact time allotted for a minilesson provides a valuable writing format for the follow-up small group work.

These examples of author web sites illustrate how two vibrant contemporary authors, T. A. Barron and Pam Muñoz Ryan, and even the deceased Roald Dahl can be invited into classrooms to provide content and inspiration for balanced literacy lesson read-aloud or write-aloud activities.

Using the author sites—with their capacity to replay the read-aloud for individual student learners, students whose native language is not English, or students from English Language Learner (ELL) families—would be wonderful for differentiating reading instruction, for teachers of ELLs and for resource room specialists.

TRY THIS WITH YOUR CLASS

Activity 1.2 Real Author Read-Aloud Marathon

Grades 1–8, Gifted and Talented

Select an author whose works you have taught to your students or whom you want them to study.

1. Check out your author's site for a read-aloud audio clip or a podcast that features the author reading from his or her work.

2. Before presenting the author's voice and expressive reading to students, have them do their own choral or individual readings.

3. Record these using a tape recorder, a digital audio recorder, or easy-to-use audio recording software with a computer (e.g., Audacity for Windows computers, GarageBand for Macs).

4. Have the class vote on which reading is the more effective and compelling oral presentation.

5. Then have students listen to the author's reading of personal work online at the author site.

6. Encourage students to react to the readings and to compare and contrast different intonations.

Just as different actors can interpret the same text with contrasting readings, all of which may be valid, so too can students and the authors differ in their spoken interpretation of various works.

Many American-born students find British author readings of their works strange, while ELLs are validated by online native language and native language speaker readings.

What is important is the introduction of the concept that reading aloud is an art form, an aspect of literacy that can include many interpretations, and a vehicle for showcasing student reader creativity. Author sites bring the real author's speaking voice into your classroom anytime.

ELLs can practice English language speaking intonations by reading aloud in the style of the real author—a fun and authentic way to learn American English pronunciations if the author is an American-born English speaker.

Guest-Inspired Shared Reading

Author sites can also be used for shared reading and guided reading activities. Shared reading can be done by teachers with small groups of students who need extra support or modeling or who want to work on reader's theater. This can be done by reading text online from any desired section of an author web site. The FAQs section available on almost every author site offers very accessible opportunities for shared reading as the teacher or student performs either the question or response part of this exchange. Built into it, if a student responds as the author, is the chance to begin to play the role of, and model, the writer. What is the main goal of balanced literacy, if it is not that?

Guided Reading

Guided reading is an approach in which the teacher reinforces skills through questioning and then discussion of a shared text. This can be nicely facilitated and "professionalized" for students (in that the professional, the author, guides the reading), as they and the teacher work with the author as virtual online mentor, by focusing on a teacher- or student-selected page of the author's web site. The selected page may be about the author's childhood and pets, interest in the environment, position on censorship, or a sampler celebrating poetry month (as on Shel Silverstein's site, www.shelsilverstein.com)— all of which make for fascinating reading and offer great human insights into the author's life and innermost priorities.

Not only does using an author site take the edge off this targeted reading comprehension skill, but it also draws teachers and students into a shared circle of online readers and writers. Focusing on the scrolling and sometimes audio-, animation-, or video-enhanced text takes such an activity many steps beyond the static, printed text and the stilted, obvious role of teacher as trainer. Using an author's web site, guided reading activities can facilitate the transformation of roles so that teacher and student become online coreading teammates working toward their mutual ongoing literacy growth.

Writing Workshop

Clearly, author sites can be used in balanced literacy lessons to great effect, allowing for some thought and previewing on the teacher's part. Within the context of the writing workshop, the teacher has to work in partnership with students to compose written products that they discuss prior to, during, and after the writing session. This can work exceptionally well with various author web sites. For example, Faith Ringgold's site (www.faith ringgold.com) includes a parable titled "How the People Became Color Blind," which she invites readers to "rewrite, illustrate, comment on, question and enjoy." This can be easily used as the prompt/schema for a shared writing or guided writing story. This model can work with a whole class or with students who need paired or small-group support.

Other authors also include beginnings of stories and poems on their sites, including Shel Silverstein's site (www.shelsilverstein.com) and Seussville (www.seussville.com). The sites of Tomie dePaola (www.tomie.com) and Jean Craighead George (www.jeancraigheadgeorge.com) provide nonfiction writing starts that also can be used for guided and shared writings. The Advice page on Pam Muñoz Ryan's site (www.pammunozryan.com) offers great opportunities for independent writing tasks or could be used for guided writing with small groups of students.

Obviously, teachers already generate their own shared writing and guided writing story/constructive action topics. But how much more engaging and authentic it is to call upon a real, famous guest author to offer suggestions for writing starts and revising works. With the use of author web sites, teachers can take students so much further. In particular, teachers and students will learn much from working with the web site of R. L. Stine and downloading his "horrific" revision unit, which includes enthralling thriller-themed genre revision exercises and the answer sheets for those exercises so that students can self-check. New teacher educators and teachers new to the formal teaching of grammar and revision will really appreciate this unit, which is a free download of the Revising Your Work section of Stine's Nightmare Room Writing Program (www.rlstine.com/swf/e1/t1/rl_classroom_kit.pdf).

If teachers and students go beyond their classroom community to respond to a published author's online prompt, they will be able to e-mail this shared writing product to the author. They can then get feedback from the author or the author's web site team. This feedback, perhaps posted on the author's site, serves to expand, concretize, and validate the notion of a virtual community of readers and writers. Students become and are literally enrolled in a virtual circle of writers.

TRY THIS WITH YOUR CLASS

Activity 1.3 Outsourced Writing Prompts and Tips

Grades 4–8, Gifted and Talented

1. Encourage students to seek out their own favorite online writing tips offered by a familiar author.

2. Display class postings of these in writing centers.

3. Give opportunities to independent student learners and those who have previously self-identified as student writers to share these prompts and their own response to them with their peers.

4. Have student writers use these favorite author site prompts to teach mini creative writing sessions to younger peers.

Phonics

Many author sites can also be used to effectively and engagingly model phonics and word use. Despite the myth that balanced literacy does not include these, they are part and parcel of the balanced literacy approach. Sites such as Seussville, the authorized Shel Silverstein site, and

Scholastic's Author and Illustrator Index (www.scholastic.com/librarians/ab/biolist.htm) include many opportunities for word play and for multimedia phonics instruction in a lively animated format that automatically captivates youngsters. Also, reading with (or after) an actual author, or famous actor who reads an author's work aloud online, can develop students' phonics and word work skills.

Literacy Centers

It is currently common and approved practice for teachers to set up literacy centers in the classroom. One center could be an author study center with task cards for the various author studies to guide students when they go online at the center. (Teachers would obviously want to preview the sites.) Teachers don't necessarily even have to make up projects, assignments, or tasks for students. They can simply direct students to various pages on specific sites and have them follow the activity there or relate the information on the site to class lessons. Best of all, students can get their writing posted on the author site or sign the guestbook there, or they can download games or activities from the sites, which can be displayed in this classroom center. Working and exploring the site in an author study or genre center will also allow students to have something to present during the sharing section of the balanced literacy lesson.

Literacy Celebrations

Another great way to use author sites is for literacy celebrations. This part of a balanced literacy approach not only represents value added but also perfectly complements the key lifelong literacy engagement goals of the approach, as well as all traditional, no-technology teaching approaches for fostering literacy. There are many ways to use author sites for literacy celebrations.

Say you want to conclude a unit celebrating an author study of Faith Ringgold. Have students who are getting ready to celebrate the unit go to her web site (www.faithring gold.com). Ask them how they could use components of the site to help decorate their classroom or gym area for the celebration. They could go through the site to get information for posters, a brochure about the author, a tour they want to give visitors to the site, music for the occasion (the site has Cassie's song), downloadable surveys (the site has a survey about racial attitudes that is appropriate for students in Grades 6 and up), and material for shared writing with Faith Ringgold that can be part of the site demonstration. Encourage students to collect quotes from the web site to post as part of the decorations for the celebration. They may want to create a timeline for her achievements (including her publications and arts exhibits) using information that is posted on her site. If possible, they may also want to download one or two pieces from her art collection, which can perhaps be used as material for a demonstration or talk during the celebration titled, for example, "Learn to Illustrate Like Faith Ringgold" or "Quilt Like Faith Ringgold" (if a student, parent, or arts educator has that expertise).

At many literacy celebrations, students costume and present themselves as either the author (if he or she has a distinct personality; e.g., T. A. Barron, Judy Blume, Eric Carle) or key characters from the author's canon (e.g., Merlin or King Arthur from T. A. Barron's adventure/fantasy series; young heroes from his *Hero's Trail*; Peter from Judy Blume's *Super Fudge* or Sheila from her *Sheila the Great*). Obviously, an author's comments and images, including photos of the author and his or her pets can tremendously inform and enhance the author characterization (check out Mary Pope Osborne and her two dogs on the Bio page of www.marypopeosborne.com).

TEACHING WITH AUTHOR WEB SITES

Document-Based Questions and Other Testing Exercises

Document-based questions (DBQs) and informational reading excerpts are currently key components of not only traditional K–8 social studies tests but also almost every standardized reading, mathematics, science, and social studies test administered in upper-elementary through middle school grades. Documents include, but are not limited to, maps, diagrams, photographs, announcements, advertisements, timelines, graphic organizers, quotes, illustrations, graphic arts, animations, and cartoons.

Check out the authorized site of any author you are studying with your students (e.g., C. S. Lewis, http://cslewis.drzeus.net; Shel Silverstein, www.shelsilverstein.com; Roald Dahl, www.roalddahl.com), and you'll find much that qualifies as material for document-based studies. Search that author by using Google or any other popular search engine, and likely a great many sites will turn up.

TRY THIS WITH YOUR CLASS

Activity 1.4 Document Author Sweep

Grades 4–8, English Language Learners

Since responding to questions about maps, diagrams, timelines, graphic organizers, and graphics/illustrations/photos is such a major focus on standardized English, science, social studies, and mathematics tests, why not immediately connect student exposure to author sites' broad array of documents by placing them in competing small groups or teams?

1. Challenge the groups you assigned for this purpose to count and categorize the documents on a particular author site (e.g., photos, illustrations, site maps, guestbook entry forms, book reviews, flyers for upcoming books or author appearances, downloadable coloring pages, activities, teacher lesson plans, suggestions for parents and librarians, articles by or about the author, author bios, publication timelines).

2. Have one student serve as recorder for the count and one as the official presenter.

3. After the teams have had a set amount of time to search through their sites to identify the broad array of potential documents, give each team a chance to present their calculation and to discuss how they classified the calculated variety of documents.

What is most exciting about this activity is that the exact number of documents on a given author site is legitimately a matter of opinion. For instance, should an item like a photo gallery count as a single document, or should you count the separate photo documents that it contains? Does a full section of text count as one document, or should it be attributed with the number representing the sum of all its components? This exercise fosters authentic student discussion and exploration of the broad number of documents on a web site.

A short exploration of a typical author web site will reveal a number of links from its home page. Following a few of these and sampling the resources that they lead to, one can't help but notice an abundant source of material to use in preparing students for the various types of texts and questions that they are required to know for standardized tests.

The site map is legitimately a document (the type that constitutes the focus of DBQ), as are other pages within the typical author site. Students can use text, graphics, and media items to study and present findings about the author's life. One might design focus questions for each section of the web site that could accomplish two teaching goals: enhancing student reading and knowledge about the specific author and improving student capacity to respond satisfactorily to specific question formats.

One approach would be to use the four-option multiple-choice format that is common on standardized tests. One could also take an author site section such as Writing Tips (a common offering on author sites) and use it for extended response, narrative account, or essay writing test practice activities. Furthermore, as one becomes familiar with a number of the web sites of various authors covered in the curriculum, using such nonfiction excerpts as the texts for targeted multiple-choice, diagram, and writing response (extended and short) questions will come naturally.

These texts, which provide more data about an author whose works students are reading, will certainly be more engaging for students than the exercises in standardized test preparation booklets, which do not have any actual curricular connection for students.

In short, teachers can easily use author web sites and their mix of graphic, chart, nonfiction, fiction, photographic, and even video content as basic texts for the creation of test format multiple-choice or essay questions. An interesting variation would involve explaining to students as a write-aloud how to use the basic texts to create specific questions intended to help them improve their scores.

Next, students can be challenged, as part of their small-group or independent work, to take excerpts from the author site text for use as questions. In other words, students become test designers using author sites—including the same images, graphics, graphic organizers, nonfiction texts, and functional/informational announcements to design their own questions. This places them in control of their test skills practice, instead of having arbitrary test questions thrown at them. Students might even upload some of these author-inspired, student-created test questions onto the site, perhaps even getting a response from the author or from other student readers who have to take the same required standardized test.

A satisfying activity like this certainly beats the tedious test skills practice that so many students currently have to endure. Figuring out if Option B on the practice exercise was the right or wrong choice clearly can't compete. Does hearing from Judy Blume (www.judyblume.com) or Pam Muñoz Ryan (www.pammunozryan.com) online in response to an e-mail posted on either of these writers' sites "successfully" demonstrate functional document test-taking skills? Absolutely, and it's accomplished in a rich, alive, author-connecting exchange. Getting an authentic response from a real author or the author's staff beats rote testing skills practice tremendously. Technology provides an empowering set of resources that makes this so. Through the use of author web sites, which are rich repositories of tech-fueled, highly motivating materials, students are engaged and teachers benefit and grow. The following chapters guide you in tapping the vast resource of author web sites.

ADDITIONAL AUTHOR SITES AND WEB RESOURCES TO EXPLORE

CLWG Children's Lit Web Guide: Authors and Illustrators on the Web

http://ucalgary.ca/~dkbrown/authors.html
   This encyclopedic index of individual author sites is a great place to start any author study.

I.N.K.: Interesting Nonfiction for Kids

http://inkrethink.blogspot.com
   This is a blog that nonfiction writers Loreen Leedy and Kathleen Krull contribute to regularly. It offers a great opportunity for students and teachers to get to know the new breed of innovative nonfiction writer's way of thinking. Gifted students in Grades 4–8 may enjoy commenting on the issues raised by the authors.

Carol Hurst's Children's Literature Site

www.carolhurst.com
   This is the premier children's K–8 multicontent, reflective, and instructional professional development site. A full two years of coursework in picture books, social studies, mathematics, science, and art themes, plus actual lesson plans and ready-to-go activities, is immediately accessible to the user. Literacy coaches, graduate education professors, and even veteran teachers can visit and revisit this one-of-a-kind treasure on the web.

HarperCollins Children's Books, Authors and Illustrators

www.harpercollinschildrens.com/kids/authorsandillustrators
   This is a collection of short, student-friendly biographical sketches of key authors published by HarperCollins. Some have links to publisher-designed author sites.

Scholastic

www2.scholastic.com
   This site contains lessons, chats, interviews, discussions, and activities for teachers. Do not miss the section for students, with its book stacks, and the one for parents.

Flamingnet

www.flamingnet.com
   These young adults' reviews of books for young adults are highly motivational for students in Grades 4–8.

Cynthia Leitich Smith

www.cynthialeitichsmith.com
   While Smith is a juvenile author, her site is an extensive resource for information on a broad spectrum of diversity, multicultural issues, and young adult authors, topics, and issues. This site is great for teacher educators, librarians, and literacy coaches.

2

Getting Started

Beginning to Explore and Use Digital Author Resources

With Eric Carle

Now that we have an overview of author sites, understand the features they generally offer, and have some ideas about how you can use them for teaching, we can expand this understanding by delving deeply into a few of the more notable and useful sites out there.

A great place to begin would be the sites of authors whose books are in use nearly ubiquitously in classrooms (e.g., Eric Carle, www .eric-carle.com). If the use of tried-

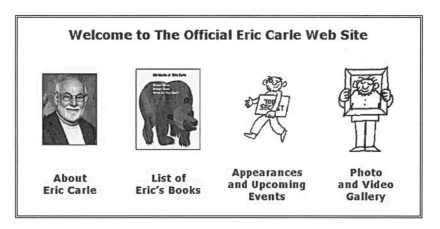

Figure 2.1 Screenshot from the home page of Eric Carle's web site

and-true print works like these can now be seen as part of a continuum of materials and learning opportunities, then it is not much of a leap to conclude that the items authors put on their web sites truly extend and enhance the content between the covers of their books.

In the cases of authors like Eric Carle—who are firmly established as producers of print work but who firmly grasp the literary value-added of a web site—we can clearly perceive the potential of this new form of instructional resource.

"It's wondrous to see how combining the old and the new create something magical." Eric Carle provided this answer in his newsletter to a question about the implantation of a computer chip into the final page of his book *The Very Quiet Cricket* (1990), providing the needed chirp for the protagonist. He uses this bit of tech magic again to produce flashers for the fireflies in *The Very Lonely Firefly* (1995). This comment demonstrates that Carle, who is over 70 years young, recognizes how technology has transformed the traditional craft of the children's book. Beyond the clever use of chips in a few of his books, however, he has masterfully tapped another, far more accessible, technology to vastly extend what he offers young readers and their teachers. His web site has become as much a part of his work as any other aspect and represents a rich trove for those who visit it.

Eric Carle is known to a generation of emergent literacy learners from Grades K–2 and beyond. Still actively creating new works, and overseeing his museum of picture book art, his time for author appearances is very limited. However, his official web site can deliver him to your classroom on demand. Many sites offer material on Carle, but the *official site* means that the author himself has developed and approved the contents of the site. Let's use Carle's site as a model to demonstrate the potential and features of this entire category of teaching and learning resources. His site has been up since 1995 and was one of the very first author sites to appear on the web. The *landing* or *home page* (shown in Figure 2.1) offers a menu of the various components to be found throughout the site. The site's resources are ready to download, print out, or show on a computer monitor (or via an LCD projector).

TRY THIS WITH YOUR CLASS

Activity 2.1 Fan Site Versus Authorized Site

Grades 4–8, Gifted and Talented

1. Tell students that Eric Carle has an authorized web site (www.eric-carle.com).

2. Share with them the fact that some popular authors have sites that are not developed with the approval of them, their estate, or their publisher, but rather are developed by their fans.

3. Show students Roald Dahl's official site (www.roalddahl.com) versus his fan site (www.roalddahlfans.com) or J. K. Rowling's official site (www.jkrowling.com) versus one of her fan sites.

4. Challenge students to take two such sites and compare/contrast their value as introductions to the author's works in a persuasive five-paragraph essay delineating the superior merits of a fan site versus an authorized author site or vice versa.

5. As an alternative, have students develop their own descriptive narratives highlighting the unique features of the fan site versus the official site.

6. For an author study exposition or an event sharing their author investigation with other classes or parents, have students develop guides and presentations to introduce their visitors to these two types of author sites.

7. For gifted and talented students, ask them to design the opening screen and setup features they would like to see on a peer student fan site for a particular author such as Eric Carle, and possibly create own their fan site using software or Web 2.0 resources (see Chapter 6). Even young learners can hand draw opening screens, features, and games on construction paper and write or word-process accompanying captions and text.

 **My Photo Albums: Childhood and family**

Figure 2.1a Snapshot from Eric Carle's online family photo album

LOOKING AT THE AUTHOR'S FAMILY ALBUM

One of the author web site resources that is always guaranteed to engage youngsters is the author's personal photo album. Eric Carle's family album, for example, is a trove of juicy discoveries (see Figure 2.1a). Teachers may find it useful to share this dimension of an author with their class first. If there's no printer in the classroom and hard-copy photos to pass around the class can't be produced, then gather students around the monitor or project the images from the site to take students on a quick tour of Carle's family album. These pictures of his family and friends make this children's literature giant seem very real, and the photographs of Carle when he was the students' age will help young learners make a strong connection with him.

READING THE AUTHOR'S BIOGRAPHY

Eric Carle's online photo albums provide a great deal of material that can make the mostly text stuff of his biography page come alive for students. The About Eric Carle section gives facts about his life and an appreciation essay about him, which is written for an adult audience. This gives the teacher a chance to learn more about Carle without rushing to the library or bookstore to get a book about him.

Teachers likely remember the traditional, routinely assigned task of researching a biography of an assigned author. The student is directed to read a whole book, a few articles, or perhaps a short section in a book of collected short biographies of authors. Frequently, the assignment would be satisfied using a standard encyclopedia entry filled with facts ready to be copied. For generations, students have dutifully copied this information, changing some words or retelling the facts they gathered in their own words. Thus, they had written a two-page biography of a selected author as part of their requirement for a research paper.

Fast-forward to the 21st century balanced literacy author study approach; everything tried and true is new again. Just as kindergarten or elementary teachers of the pretechnology era read aloud to students, perhaps from an author biography, today's teachers can have information read aloud to them from Eric Carle's bio on the web, an act that models for millennial students the connection between text reading and the exciting new intellectual life to be had on the web.

Just as yesterday's teachers framed questions about an author biography (as well as about the accompanying photos) based on the text being read in class, today's teachers can prescreen an author site to generate appropriate questions to focus student comprehension and attention to biographical author details.

TRY THIS WITH YOUR CLASS

Activity 2.2 All About Me: My Own Author Bio

All Grades, English Language Learners, and Gifted and Talented

Eric Carle's web site has a particularly effective author bio that includes photos and personal details about his childhood, interests, travels, awards, and more. Most author sites include bios of different lengths that are shared through images or in text that uses a conversational tone.

1. Have students of all grade levels—authors of their own creative writings—use author web site bios as templates for designing their own "all about me" bios.

2. Download and print out from these sites author bios for students to examine and use as they write and illustrate their own bios following the layout of the author site.

3. For more mature upper-elementary learners, have students investigate various favorite or class-assigned author sites to find one whose bio format most appeals to them. Then they can style their own bios after these.

4. Ask students to provide a short explanation of why they selected a particular author site format and how their bio conforms to the template.

5. If your classes can add content to the school's web site, have students create a page of Classroom Author Bios or display their bios when the class desktop publishes them.

POSING QUESTIONS AND MAKING CONNECTIONS FOR UNDERSTANDING

Author web site resources can help forge great connections between reading and understanding, especially when effective questions are posed to students by their teachers, who guide them to and through these sites. The following are a few sample questions that have worked well for this purpose with early elementary students:

- What did Eric Carle look like when he was your age?
- What was his house like?
- Where did he go to school?
- Who was in his family?

A common prereading practice for emergent readers is to prompt them to imagine the author, what he's like, the details of his life, and his motivations for and approaches to writing. As they read, most readers, and certainly most young readers, create a mental picture of the author as a child. Every reader looks at the author's picture on the book jacket.

Once students have created their own childhood of imagined pictures of Eric Carle, they can go to his site and click on Childhood and Family (under Photo and Video Gallery) to see the actual photos from that period in Carle's life. They can then compare and contrast them to the ones they created in their minds. As all teachers of young children know, many children as they are inculcated into the habits of lifelong literacy love nothing more than to visit and revisit favorite books and images. They can display their imagined pictures of Carle as a peer, next to printouts from this page of the site, or revisit this favorite page whenever they like.

Carle, by virtue of his longevity as a favorite children's author, his international background (he spent many years in Germany), and his rich cultural/historical lifespan, has gone through many different image changes with some distinctive physical identifying features that delight his readers of all ages. Ask the students which character of Carle's they feel most looks like or includes the features of the author, even if it is an animal or insect family member. Remember, many artists draw on their own facial characteristics, even bringing them into their animal character creations. After they have fun identifying what might be Carle's features on *The Very Hungry Caterpillar* (1969) or *Mister Seahorse* (2004), they can then check out the many faces of Carle to be found on his site (in the photos and videos).

Children might want to spot and share their own Eric Carle "lookalike" sightings in their neighborhood. They can enjoy sharing these directly on Carle's site as part of their guestbook entries. Or they can be on the lookout for actual pictures of Carle in the news, in children's magazines, or on other web sites (e.g., his Museum of Picture Book Art).

Teachers and students alike will find Carle's Friends and Colleagues photo album interesting, particularly if they are involved in reading the works of a variety of authors. Here, they'll catch glimpses of Carle with other famous authors, and with and without his beard. Carle's *prebeard* and *with beard* photos are always of tremendous interest to younger readers.

MAKING ART: A PROCEDURAL ACCOUNT

Carle's site offers some rich, child-friendly material. For example, there's "How I create my pictures" (see Figure 2.2). This exciting section has Carle himself demonstrating and giving a procedural account, an aspect of balanced literacy writing that's very challenging to teach. He personally gives his readers a photographic, sequenced, demonstration of his process. Step by step, he shows how the process of his art technique unfolds. Even when a teacher does manage to invite an author or illustrator into the classroom for a one-shot appearance

How I create my pictures

Draw a caterpillar onto tracing paper or other transparent paper.

Figure 2.2 Screenshot from a slide show on Eric Carle's web site

or ongoing residency, it is unlikely that the author or illustrator could provide students with as perfectly staged and presented an experience as this slide show of the illustration process on Carle's site.

Even if students can't follow all the details of the process, it's there for them to reflect on and try to comprehend. This is true as well for teachers who, unless they are arts educators, may not fully understand the process. However, this online modeling serves to make both teachers and students part of Carle's insiders' circle of "knowing" readers. Whatever the nature or content, such a connection between author and reader is a great step forward for literacy learners.

A particularly valuable dimension to web sites like Eric Carle's is that the resources they contain can be presented to students (or accessed by them directly) over and over. Students love to see something again and again, and being able to do so is especially valuable for students who are spatially oriented (learning style/multiple intelligence), have special needs, or are learning English as a second language. Such resources are also great for independent reading, small-group collaborative work, or for use in teacher-student conferencing. They provide something to share that easily breaks the tension of such situations, thereby destressing informal assessments.

It is often difficult for early childhood literacy learners to conceive the connections between the story, the storyteller, and/or the artist/illustrator, even when, as is the case of Eric Carle, all three are rolled up into one charismatic individual. Using his site's slide shows immediately makes accessible to all learners, no matter what their dominant learning style, the roles that Carle plays in creating the various dimensions of his books. Through his Photo and Video Gallery, Carle comes into the classroom to model his writing approach for students. Teachers can individualize instruction through the use of his slide shows to motivate students who, whether because of learning style, intelligence strength, special needs, or English Language Learner (ELL) background, respond differently to the powerful story narratives or rhythmic patterns. These media items make visual art accessible to readers and, of course, are available for students who want to focus on Carle as illustrator and artist.

And even better than a live demonstration at his Museum of Picture Art or at a local school or a bookstore, Carle's web-based slide shows can be repeated on demand for review or simply for the sheer joy of watching him share his work. Learners may concentrate on different dimensions and details with each viewing, perhaps returning to this source of inspiration after attempting personal work, making comparisons between the products and processes of virtual mentor and learning apprentice.

MODELING OF PROCEDURAL WRITING

Carle also models procedural-account writing through slide shows on his site. This gives teachers the opportunity to provide especially rich examples of procedural-account writing and reading by having students compare and contrast a number of sterling and unique examples. For instance, Carle's methodology for producing collage art (used for most of his works) can be compared and contrasted with approaches and techniques he used for his book *Mister Seahorse*. His slide shows support such analysis and comparison wonderfully.

Through class read-alouds of Carle's works, and viewing his online photo albums, students can be inspired to try their hand at storytelling, too. Carle's modeling of his picture creation and collage design process can help motivate and inform students in becoming pictorial storytellers for whom (depending on their kinesthetic and spatial learning entry points) the art may precede or supersede the words. Carle's web site, with its many writer's craft ideas and the showcased videos and photos, automatically accommodates a variety of learning styles.

By looking at Carle's step-by-step process modeling, children can become confident Carle-style picture and collage makers. Even better, the coupling of the slides or photos with the process can provide a spatial entry point for them and a model for using his procedural account to write other procedural accounts. One of the many books Carle has produced is *Pancakes, Pancakes!* (1970), another perfect model to use in helping children with procedural accounts.

TRY THIS WITH YOUR CLASS

Activity 2.3 How I Make My Art!

Grades 2–8, English Language Learners, and Gifted and Talented

One of the most powerful components of Eric Carle's site, and that of other illustrator/authors, is the video and slide show presentations that he includes detailing his step-by-step processes. These get to the essence of the standards-mandated narrative account procedure, which students have to be able to

(Continued)

(Continued)

communicate in speech and writing. Seeing and hearing favorite authors such as Carle communicate their steps can make this sequential required talking, direction following, and writing format real for students.

1. Have students review Carle's videos and slide shows or similar items on other author/illustrator web sites.

2. After several viewings, ask students to detail as individuals or as a class how they do a particular art project of their own, whether it be building a model, making a portrait, or sketching what happens outside their window.

3. For ELLs, the visualization of the art process authenticates English narrative procedure. Ask them to discuss or share narrative account procedure for a native background art form, such as Matryoshka dolls or Chinese brush painting.

4. Have ELLs explain the process in their native language or do a translation of Carle's or other authors' videos into their native language.

VISITING THE AUTHOR'S STUDIO

My Photo Albums: My Studio

Figure 2.3 Screenshot of Eric Carle in his studio, from the author's web site

Carle's site has a photo album called My Studio, which is an invitation to readers to examine his personal space (see Figure 2.3). "Welcome to where I work," Carle seems to say to his site visitors as they eavesdrop on him at work in his studio. This is an opportunity for teachers to create an excellent modeled writing minilesson. It also illustrates a general approach to using functional sections of author sites to create valuable authentic experiences for students.

CREATING A WRITING MINILESSON

Before students view the My Studio album on Carle's site, ask them to imagine and discuss or draw answers to the following prompts:

- Where do you imagine the author Eric Carle writes and draws his stories?
- Does he write in a kitchen? Does he write in a classroom like ours? Does he have an office like the principal's or the doctor's or your parent's where he goes everyday to write his stories or create his art?

If students come up with the idea that an artist has a special room or space where he goes to do work, share with them the term *artist's studio* and then challenge them to come up with what an artist's studio, particularly for an author such as Carle, would look like. Model what they might come up with in terms of objects, materials, posters, and just plain "stuff" that Carle would need in order to design a particular book, say *Mister Seahorse*. As part of the minilesson, provide numerous opportunities and sufficient time for students to come up with a drawing and a verbal description of what Carle's studio might contain.

By this point in the students' author study of Carle's works and tour of his site, they have already seen him creating his art and collages, step-by-step (via the procedural account narratives in his slide shows). Therefore, you can refer students back to the slide shows or even revisit them online together so that they can glimpse and revisit these scenes from Carle's studio, which is of course the site for these demonstrations.

As in all student-driven, teacher-modeled writing minilessons, the key is to have students begin to talk about and provide sentence descriptions of Carle's studio based on their readings of his works, their tour of his author site up to this point, and their own judgments of what an artist's studio space should contain.

With a good two-thirds or more input from students, develop at least a three- to four-sentence description of Carle's studio on the chalk/whiteboard or chart paper (for a second- or third-grade class) and have a somewhat finished illustration of the studio (completed almost entirely by students or a single student artist) by the conclusion of the minilesson in modeled writing. With this material as the foundation, students can be broken up into small groups to develop their own written and sketched visions of Carle's studio as an outgrowth of the whole-group modeling. After they have completed their small-group work, they can return to the sharing portion of the balanced literacy lesson, each group offering their own descriptions of Carle's studio and accompanying illustration to reflect those written descriptions.

After all students have finished sharing their writings and illustrations of Carle's studio, have them accept Carle's gracious invitation to visit his studio. As they tour the real studio, perhaps facilitated by the teacher or librarian, they can compare and contrast their descriptions and drawings with the real thing, as seen on his site.

Among the possible discussion topics suggested by a critical review of these sections of Carle's site is his illustration-driven writing process based on actual photos showing him painting his tissue papers. These photos convey the hard work, meticulousness, and intensity of effort that yields a single picture book.

One photo on Carle's site documents the research he does to accurately convey his deliberately small creatures—fireflies, caterpillars, seahorses, and others—by referencing a collection of reference books stored on shelves in his study. It might be interesting and challenging as part of independent research for a Carle author study to have students select one or two favorite Carle works and then consider what kinds of books about the subject of the work or the art collage process Carle might have used in his research for that work. The independent student researcher or small group of researchers can decide on a number of nonfiction books on subjects such as insects or caterpillars and then write paragraphs about each book, explaining why it might have been useful to Carle in his research for past books or might inspire him to develop new books. This activity can be fueled and supported by search engine–based inquiries, with students logging the items turned up on the web and annotating their usefulness.

Students can share these descriptions of potentially good research reads for Carle with other class members, but more important, they can send their identified finds to Carle to see whether these titles were indeed ones he used or plans to use based on their recommendation. They can do this by using his web site's guestbook, directly e-mailing him, or sending him their annotated lists via snail mail. Obviously, such activities are to be supervised and guided by the school or district Internet acceptable use policy.

What is particularly rich about the design of Carle's site, and the balanced literacy writing workshop lessons that can be developed from it, is that the virtual tour of his studio allows the teacher to use standard writer's workshop prompts and then direct students to use site resources to check and confirm the real-life accuracy of their classroom responses. Without the author site to reference at the end of the response, the exercises are only purposeful and useful for critical thinking, reading, and descriptive writing skills development in the abstract. However, by using the actual online studio and art-making process included on Carle's site, you can ensure that students' products in response to them can be validated by Carle's real studio. Use of the online studio makes that validation as immediate and as repeatable as clicking on My Studio. This feature allows you to engage both spatial learners and verbal learners in a check-and-confirm descriptive writing exercise that enhances a Carle author study.

TRY THIS WITH YOUR CLASS

Activity 2.4 Using Video to Show the Art Process

Grades 2–5

1. If a video camera is available, have students create their own step-by-step "How We Make Art" videos in the style of Eric Carle and other illustrators.

2. As an alternative, have students simply string a series of still images together and import them into user-friendly, ubiquitously available video software (e.g., Windows Movie Maker for Windows machines, iMovie for Macs). The web abounds with how-to tutorials on using this software for those who need a little support (see also Chapter 6).

3. After the still images are in place, have students use the software to add titles, text, and/or spoken narration.

4. For students who identify themselves as authors or comic book designers, encourage them to make parallel videos of their own writing or illustrating process, using the formats of the author videos as a template.

5. Suggest that students who enjoy acting dress up as the author in the web video and demonstrate his or her art process. This would utilize author web site material to engage auditory, linguistic, and interpersonal learners as well as enhance spoken language skills.

CONSULTING FREQUENTLY ASKED QUESTIONS

Like its creator, Carle's web site was ahead of the children's author/illustrator pack. Because of his popularity and resulting contact and conversations with an appreciative and verbal audience, he decided to develop what is one of the finest Frequently Asked Questions (FAQ) sections on this type of site.

Developing the Traditional List of Author Study Questions

One of the key components of an evolving author study, as the balanced literacy approach conceptualizes it, is the generation of a series of questions by the whole class. These are questions that students have about the author and his or her works, which they hope to answer by the end of their study. This well-established approach is often used by traditional teachers of reading who want their classes to study multiple works by a single author.

Generally, this approach is done as a whole-group brainstorming activity after students have read at least two works by the same author. Students are prompted, as part of an author study minilesson, to generate a broad range of questions about the author and his or her works, characters, and sometimes issues or concerns that are important to the author. Among these concerns might be family, values, the environment, animal life, the natural world, citizenship, and cultural differences.

To focus students' readings of the author's works, generally encourage them to brainstorm as many questions as they can for the various aspects of the author's life and chief writing/social concerns. Students then write down these questions, along with the date, and reference them throughout the author study. Often, as students identify information or responses that provide answers to particular questions, a report, brief annotation, or check is made for that question and some form of visual posting or project (e.g., poster, experiential chart) is displayed. This becomes part of the sharing portion of the author study.

Interestingly, now that the author site has been established as a common practice among writers and illustrators, the FAQs section of such a site comes into play as literacy educators assimilate the resources of the Web into longstanding traditions of practice and approach.

Connecting Author Study Questions With FAQs

The FAQs on Eric Carle's site is a mother lode of all kinds of questions from students and adults about his published and growing work. Carle includes his wonderful hand-drawn illustrations within the design of each question. Clicking on any of the questions causes a succinct response to pop up that is genuinely the author's and is extremely accessible to young readers.

How might you connect this feature of Carle's site with the author study questions that students came up with in the brainstorming excise? When doing the usual classroom introduction for the author study, which it is best to do right after students have heard and studied two or more of Carle's works, ask students to generate a series of questions that they would like to ask Carle about his works. Here are some typical classroom responses that one would expect to such a prompt:

- Why did you write about a caterpillar?
- How do you make your pictures?
- How long does it take to write a book?
- Do you first draw pictures and then tell the story?
- What was the first story you wrote?
- How did you make the spider web in *The Very Busy Spider?*
- What book is your favorite? Why?

Write the students' questions as an experience chart, and post it in a prominent location in the classroom. This is standard ritual for an author study. However, using the FAQs from the author's official web site allows for a richer experience. Inform students that they are going to get to meet Eric Carle at his virtual home. (This is an alternative way to introduce students to web-based author study, instead of beginning by visiting Carle's photo album, as suggested earlier in the chapter.) Whether you are controlling a single computer viewed by all through the use of an LCD projector or students are in a lab or other situation in which there is one-to-one computer access, you can deepen the ritual and embed some technology skills learning here by making the typing of the URL and navigation of the site part of the activity's formal process.

The result will be students who are delighted to see Carle's site, with its trademark and recognizable (to them, as Carle readers) iconic caterpillar and ladybug animation, appear on screen. Students will indeed feel welcome as the "Welcome to the Official Eric Carle Web Site" message comes into view.

Next, students examine the home page, discussing which of its features matches up with stuff they have been talking about as part of their author study. Once they notice the FAQs, explain that at his official web site, Carle receives lots of e-mail questions, just as students themselves receive snail mail and e-mail. Once they understand this step, do a read-aloud or a guided or interactive reading minilesson (depending on the students' reading abilities), with the students scrolling through the questions as they appear and clicking on the answers or selected questions.

For small-group activities, students can select either specific questions and answers that they want to explore or check out the questions that correspond to those that they raised when they developed their author study question list. Make sure that, whichever the prompt chosen for them to follow, students have plenty of time to scroll through and read on their own or with help. It is also a good idea to target students' small-group exploration of this component of the web site by telling them that they will have to do a presentation about their findings during the sharing portion of the balanced literacy lesson.

Make certain that during the sharing portion of the lesson, each small group not only shares Carle's response to the FAQs, but also has the opportunity to react as readers to those responses. Encourage not only each individual group, but also the whole class to talk about Carle's responses. Write down further questions or interesting comments that students make in response to the conversation about Carle's answers to the FAQs. Make certain that each student who comments is credited with a specific comment.

If one small group or some independent learners have chosen to compare and contrast the FAQs posted on the web site with their own list of questions, give them a chance to sum up their findings with, perhaps, checks placed on the poster next to the questions they asked that are answered on Carle's site. Have them then react to Carle's answers for these questions by explaining whether they, as readers and as class questioners, find the answers satisfying. Give them a chance to make their own reaction comments, and then post these and credit the students by name with their quotes.

Next, have the whole class reflect on and respond to why some of their class questions appear in the FAQs on Carle's web site. Emphasize that this crossover between their questions and those asked frequently by other Carle readers makes your students a viable part of Carle's virtual community of readers, connected by their admiration for his stories and the web.

Give students the chance to discuss which of their questions does not appear on Carle's FAQs and why these may not have been raised yet by other readers. Again, be certain to record the distinctive remarks of students who offer comments in this discussion.

TRY THIS WITH YOUR CLASS

Activity 2.5 Focusing on Science and Art FAQs

Grades 2–5

1. Have students focus on Eric Carle's FAQs that are about the science or the art techniques behind his stories (e.g., why the butterfly in *The Very Hungry Caterpillar* comes from a cocoon, not a chrysalis; why *Mister Seahorse* looks different from book to book).

2. Once students have examined these FAQs, encourage them to generate more questions about the marine and insect science aspects of Carle's works or his art techniques.

3. Depending on their reading and research ability, and their capacity to use the Internet, ask students to generate answers to some of their science and art questions.

4. Encourage students to e-mail their responses to their own FAQ-inspired questions to Carle for use in the Caterpillar Express newsletter or to be posted on the Caterpillar Express bulletin board.

As a Follow-Up to the Lesson

The fruits of Activity 2.5 can be submitted to Carle's web site via the Guestbook and Contact section. It is quite likely that the class will receive a reply. Even if a reply is not received in a timely fashion, the act of formulating and sending the message is a wonderful, empowering, focused, authentic literacy experience for students.

As a practical matter, it may be advantageous for you to do the actual e-mailing or filling out the guestbook entry. However, having students prepare their message by typing, with perhaps some correction and revision, will increase their sense of participation and ownership. Even in second and third grades, it may be possible for children to peck away or even laboriously type their own comments. If this is the case, allow them to do so, because then they will truly have ownership of their communication with this revered author. The e-mail response that the class receives will be an invaluable living connection with the author, one kinesthetically as well as verbally owned by students.

Teachers of elementary school students are always focused instilling these crucial, life-changing habits so that students can join the circle of lifelong readers. Signing Carle's guestbook, seeing their comment in the guestbook, e-mailing him and then getting his response—these foster a lifelong literacy habit of communicating directly with an author and that author's readers.

ADDITIONAL AUTHOR SITES AND WEB RESOURCES TO EXPLORE

Special Section: Celebrity Author Fan Sites

As classes pursue their favorite authors across the web, they'll inevitably discover some of the fan sites of extremely well-known "celebrity" authors. These sites reveal the world of literary stardom, a great motivator for literacy learning, and can inspire students to read more intensely. Check out these examples of celebrity author fan sites:

Judy Blume's mailing address:

www.fanmail.biz/73108.html

Proof that Faith Ringgold is a Hollywood star:

www.hollywood.com/celebrity/Faith_Ringgold/1497110

Chris Van Allsburg, who has had several of his children's books made into Hollywood movies, is also a star:

www.hollywood.com/celebrity/chrisvan_allsburg/1574079

Fans often like to weigh in on the impact authors have had on their reading and personal lives. Such online submissions can be great, authentic response-to-literature writing activities for students and even the inspiration and model for class author study projects in Grade 4–8. For example, here is a fan response to Judy Blume's ongoing body of work:

http://popwatch.ew.com/popwatch/2008/09/judy-blume-memo.html

While J. K. Rowling has a terrific authorized web site, her legions of fans can also enjoy and compare and contrast the material on the Muggle Net Fan site (Grades 4–8):

www.mugglenet.com

3

Reading Through Writing

Rich Language Arts and Social Studies Learning

With T. A. Barron

I n Eric Carle's site we found key ways to extend and enhance the print book experience for students. The continuum of literacy activities may begin with either a book or a web site, but it is in the body of print works and the many types of materials on a web site that the richest and, in this day and age, most relevant types of experiences are to be had. Carle's work, and that of authors whose work is similar, is clearly applicable for young students. However, there is nothing about the author site approach that is limited to students of this age or the types of activities teachers commonly use to engage them.

The next two authors and their sites that we will focus on—T. A. Barron in this chapter and Judy Blume in Chapter 4—clearly illustrate the applicability of author sites and the resources they offer across grade and age levels. And while some features and components are

Figure 3.1 Screenshot from T. A. Barron's web site

similar to those found on Carle's site (e.g., biographical information) older students can be engaged in ways that are appropriate for their age group. Furthermore, these sites introduce other types of content and activities especially for older students: character education through reflection on the qualities of heroes in Barron's case, and in the case of Blume, social activism and the need for it as reflected in her concern and writing about censorship.

Barron is a juvenile trade book author whose broad spectrum of works present themes of fantasy, adventure, nature, individual heroism, and environmental concerns. The purposeful design of his author site makes it one of the key ways he communicates with his growing audience. The site and its many resources can provide much for in-depth implementation of the reading and writing workshop on a middle school level.

TRY THIS WITH YOUR CLASS

Activity 3.1 Getting the Word Out:
Middle School Authors Also Write for Young Children

Grades 4–8, Gifted and Talented

Many middle school students are unaware that some of their favorite authors (e.g., T. A. Barron, www.tabarron.com; Judy Blume, www.judyblume.com; Gary Soto, www.garysoto.com) also write for younger readers.

1. Challenge students who explore these and other sites to identify so-called teen authors who also write for younger kids.

2. Have students compile an annotated list of such authors and their titles in a poster or document that can be posted online.

3. Arrange for them to share this list with younger siblings and peers, elementary grade librarians, parents, and teachers.

4. Encourage students to send their annotated poster or document to the authors.

Students who spread the word in this way are also using research and functional literacy skills to authentically expand authors' readership and to share the wealth of literacy with a set of new, younger readers—a functional and informational literacy win-win-win.

MAPPING OUT READING AND WRITING WORKSHOP CONNECTIONS

True to Barron's comment about his web site being "a travel brochure for the imagination," his works are full of maps. Why would he be involved so intensely with maps if he is primarily famous for his fantasy and adventure middle-grade stories? A major focus currently in middle school writing classrooms across the country is to engage students in studying travel brochures and guide books as reading genres. Ironically, if Barron's work was nonfiction, he would provide perfect examples and models for informational brochure assignments for middle school students. The next reading-through-writing step of the process, after examining and analyzing examples, is to have students produce their own informational brochures about various states and countries. An unusual and worthwhile connection to Barron's wilderness books would be to use them for these social studies reading-through-writing projects.

Interpreting and Follow-Up Writing

Many times in middle school and upper elementary grades, students are asked to correctly interpret a map and must answer questions using a map as the key source document. When connected to a fictional, so-called fantasy book, this activity can be an especially rich experience, with wonderful possibilities for supporting and nurturing students' descriptive writing and paragraph formation skills as well as key geography and map social studies skills.

How does an emphasis on mapping on Barron's web site help you map out informational, directional, descriptive, and informational writing tasks? Under the Maps section of his site (which you can get to via the Explorations tab), click on the Avalon Map and use it with Activity 3.2. Note that this was drawn by the author himself.

TRY THIS WITH YOUR CLASS

Activity 3.2 Applying Barron's Map Idea

Grades 1–2

1. Have children select a favorite story to map.

2. Help them map out the story, even if the characters only move from one room to another or one house in a village to another, or ask them to work independently.

3. Alternately, have students create a map of their movement throughout the school day.

4. Students can then develop stories or reading exercises for peer classes that include the use of maps.

Students might be directed to write out their own directions to a particular site in the realms of Barron's *The Great Tree of Avalon*. They could organize a set of bulleted directions to follow sequentially to travel from one place to another within the realms. This would teach and enhance the interpretation of informational documents, a key reading skill. And assigning students to write a set of directions for traveling from one place in the realm to another in the least time-consuming way would involve them in producing a procedural account. They would enjoy doing that straight off the web site. The activity could then be connected with the book and the beauty of the map that Barron developed.

An interesting technology extension of this idea involves having students study how online map tools like MapQuest and Google Maps generate and display travel directions between two places, and then create their own version for places within the worlds created by Barron. Additionally, as part of their independent informational and fiction reading, students could design their own maps for specific neighborhoods and regions described in nonfiction and fiction works. Of course, they would have to reference their maps to the material that they had read, whether online or in print, and write one or more paragraphs explaining their design. In the process of creating this persuasive paragraph(s), they would have to cite details from their reading to support the different design elements of the maps they developed. They would also need to integrate various elements of topographic representation and other map terms that they studied. This assignment would be a great opportunity for students with mathematical, spatial, kinesthetic, interpersonal, and other learning strengths (beyond auditory and linguistic) to contribute their various talents for a reading-through-writing project.

Teachers can also use the maps on Barron's web site in other ways. After the students study the maps, ask them to do the following:

- Develop a storyline of their own, involving one or more places on the map.
- Write a detailed description of what a setting like "The Haunted Marsh" or "The Legendary Isle of Fincarya" might look like if they journeyed there on foot.
- Create poetry or interior monologues told from the perspectives of explorers and adventurers.

Using maps as an anticipatory exercise can highly motivate students to read T. A. Barron's books, since in exploring and navigating the fictive terrain to develop their own routes, they will want to learn about the routes he deliberately includes in his writings.

TRY THIS WITH YOUR CLASS

Activity 3.3 Multicultural Myth Maps: Making Multicultural/Historical Fiction Connections

Grades 4–5, English Language Learners, Gifted and Talented, and Avid Readers

T. A. Barron has chosen to focus his historical fiction writing and map designs on the Merlin era of English folklore. But there are other history-based fictional legends rooted in the traditions of Russia, France, Kenya, South Africa, the Congo, Egypt, Saudi Arabia, Mexico, and other countries. Students from families who have recently immigrated have a ready source of foreign language maps and personal family/community stories on which to draw.

1. Have students apply Barron's emphasis on mapping his historical fiction trilogies to another region and culture.

2. Ask them to create maps for the books of another historical fiction writer whose work they admire.

3. Encourage them to share their responses with this author and his or her web site.

4. Alternatively, have students develop a two-page preview of their own historical fiction idea based on independent reading or family stories.

This activity values the personal experiences and family/cultural resources of the English Language Learners (ELLs) and offers avid independent readers a chance to shine.

Games as Test Practice

T. A. Barron's site has more features for educators and students that are relevant to testing. Click on Games (also under the Explorations tab), and you find questions that have three-option responses and relate to the narratives of the books. Although these are called "games" by Barron, they provide document-based standardized test practice for students. You could even use some of the questions as part of an independent author study of Barron by adding in a fourth answer so that the format would parallel most of the standardized social studies and English language arts tests that students have to take every year.

After students play a game, they have the option of sending their responses to Barron via his web site. In addition, by completing a form, they can get on his mailing list and receive his newsletter. By correctly filling out this form and successfully submitting it online, students are demonstrating their functional document reading and writing skills for an authentic purpose with actual feedback from an author's web site.

To extend the activity, students might be asked to create their own games for their mapping of other fictional and nonfictional works they have read.

TRY THIS WITH YOUR CLASS

Activity 3.4 Go Geography Creative

Grades 1–8

Designing board games inspired by maps from T. A. Barron's or other map-evocative texts engages learners of various styles, including kinesthetic, visual, and problem solvers, in a literacy-inspired shared enterprise that has its roots in the texts and illustrations of print books.

1. Help younger students, kinesthetic learners, and ELLs create map board games.

2. Have them use cards that detail clues or vocabulary from Barron's picture books.

3. Encourage students to photograph or scan their board game formats and submit them for sharing on his site.

Since Barron's site does not currently have map games from his works for young children, this will provide a needed resource. In creating these maps, young learners are becoming document-based insiders who know how to respond to test questions about maps, which are used on all key standardized tests.

INSPIRING NEW WRITERS

Explicit Writing Workshop Prompts

T. A. Barron views his web site as a place to inspire what he terms "new writers." When you check out his site, you find some insightful statements about the craft of writing, like this one from the Welcome section of the Meet T. A. Barron page (see Figure 3.2): "Writing is both the most joyous—and most agonizing—labor I know. And it is by far the best way to travel—in our world or any other." This is a wonderful quote for student writers to reflect on. They can discuss it by sharing their own insights and list it alongside other quotes they find online from authors they admire and who they feel have good advice to share with students.

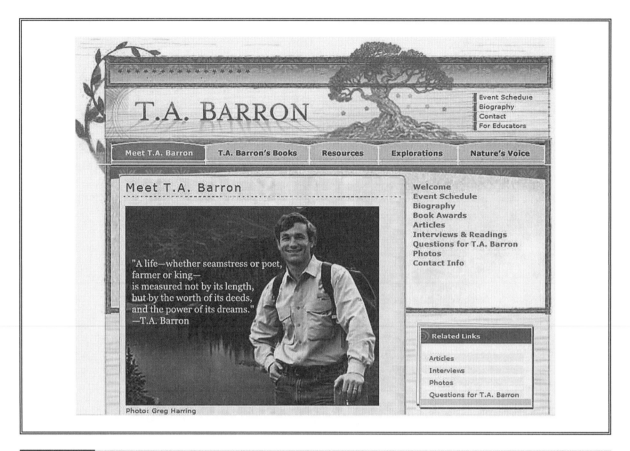

Figure 3.2   Screenshot of the Meet T. A. Barron page

TRY THIS WITH YOUR CLASS

Activity 3.5 Writers' Words to Remember: Quoting T. A. Barron and Other Authors

Grades 4–8

As noted, many authors include writing prompts on their web sites, and offer direct comments about their writing process and tips to young writers. Drawing on these comments, students can create classroom display placards or posters, a treasury of comments, or a calendar.

1. Working as a class, in small groups, or as independent readers, students review the web sites of T. A. Barron and other authors to identify as many quotes as they can that they like and that inspire them in their own writing.

2. As a beginning task, assign students to find at least 5–10 quotes on the theme of writing, to be included on a poster.

3. Have them illustrate the quotes for their posters or use fancy word-processing techniques (like Word Art) to turn the text of the quotes into designs.

4. Hang the posters in the classroom, hall displays, or school library.

5. As an alternative project, have students take individual quotes on writing and make placards with illustrations or downloaded author/character images on them to serve as classroom/writing center displays or border designs for posted student writings.

6. If you want to focus intensively on the writing process and have students work with quotes as nonfiction text excerpts for discussion and analysis, broaden the task so that each student has to look online to find 5–7 quotes about writing.

7. Have them explain in a sentence or more why these quotes are useful for readers and writers.

8. To extend the project for avid readers and/or gifted and talented students, have them share their work with the whole class. A reasonable number of quotes, say 50, can be set for such learners.

The final products from this activity can include a Writer's Quote of the Day to be included in the school calendar or distributed as gift calendars. These can include names of the student researchers, their commentary about the quotes, and perhaps illustrations. The calendars can be desktop published, photocopied, and bound (many copy shops offer binding service at a modest cost) and then distributed throughout the school community. Or the finished piece can be uploaded as a feature on the class or school web site.

Barron boils down his advice to three key words: observe, practice, and believe. Students love short directions, and this advice is immensely deep and full of possibilities. In fact, every phrase in the short descriptive paragraphs found in Barron's books could become a single writing prompt or an extensive assignment or project to help not only with author study in particular, but also generally with teaching reading through writing skills.

The writing prompts Barron offers go beyond English language arts or even social studies/history content, which is the limit one might expect of them because of his Arthurian myth trilogy series. But writing based on Barron's stories can also incorporate, for instance, science observation and data collection skills, competencies that are difficult to teach.

TRY THIS WITH YOUR CLASS

Activity 3.6 Writing Tips From Other Cultures

Grades 4–8

Expand Activity 3.5 to writers who were not born in the United States or who deliberately bring their non-American cultural experiences to the writing process. This activity allows students to focus on writers of multicultural literature, whose traditions and values offer everyone in the class a new perspective on writing, and it affirms for ELLs the ways in which other cultures inspire authors and illustrators as they write for American audiences.

If ELLs are able to reproduce and share a writer's insights in both their native language and English, then this investigation will be doubly rewarding and can, of course, also be shared in middle school foreign language classes.

The Writing Process

"How do different types of trees' leaves fall to the ground, each with a singular sort of flight?" In his tips For Aspiring Writers, Barron beautifully and aptly suggests that young writers think of writing as growing a tree and then explains how he begins with a seed, outlines its growth, watches it grow into a sapling, and then is guided by the tree it has become. Ultimately, his rewrites help him "shape the growing tree." After this shaping, Barron is ready to submit the piece to his editor.

What is lovely about his very science-grounded description of his writing process is how powerfully and wonderfully it parallels the steps in the writing process: prewriting/ brainstorming, writing, revising, editing, and publishing. What is also authentic, as delivered by an obviously accomplished author, is how long it takes to produce a book from start to finish. In Barron's case, this is between one and three years.

Especially important advice to young writers is what he says about rewrites. He says that he spends "as much [time] as it takes to get it right. . . . [T]here is no substitute for the integrating and deepening that happens in a thorough rewrite." This type of comment can and should be shared with students. They should be encouraged to write to him and express their own feelings on this issue. Students are always eager to finish their revision and be done with their work, as are many adult authors, who demonstrate the same impatience and reluctance to revise.

Truth in Fiction

Barron's *The Lost Years of Merlin* epic has won many fans, both juvenile and adult. Clearly, his works on Merlin (of Arthurian legend) involve much historical research and required extensive reading in primary and secondary sources from that time period. On the For Aspiring Writers page, Barron explains that he does research "to make the story's characters and places feel true. For that is the ultimate test: Good fiction is true on many levels. . . . Fiction must feel true. On the levels of the senses, the emotions, the intellect, and the soul, a story ought to win the reader's belief."

This statement provides an excellent opportunity for students to reflect on the research and truth in fiction. They can take time not only to comment on Barron's works, but also to reflect and write persuasively on the truths behind many of their favorite works of fiction in that these successful works generally resonate with the student readers' lives and experiences. That is why certain fiction books become classics—their characters and situations are true for a large community of readers. Skilled educators can demonstrate to students the truth in selected works of fiction.

Related is Barron's comment about writing a biographical sketch of a character to get to know the character better. This task offers another rich core reading-through-writing option for students (and adults as well) that targets their detailed reading and comprehension and taps their creativity and sensitivity to character voice. A biographical writing exercise can be used with almost any fiction or even nonfiction character (although in the case of nonfiction, students should research and digest the real person's biography).

Believe in Yourself

One of the most striking of T. A. Barron's tips is his focus on "believe," one of his three key governing principles. This charge to writers is inherently one that builds self-esteem and is self-empowering. It is obvious from his explanation of this principle for effective writing that Barron, although not a current or former professional teacher of writing for middle or high school students, believes that the mind-set and confidence of the writer is of crucial importance to all writers' success. He notes: "To succeed, you must truly believe in your story. . . . [Y]ou must believe in yourself. Know that you have valuable things to say, and the skills to say them; know that your song is unique, that your voice matters."

This quotation can be used as a document and connected to the key practice of document-based questioning (linking two documents through connecting questions), to the student's own work, or with the student's evaluation of other authors' degree of confidence in their own works and their abilities to tell their stories or get their messages across.

Certainly, we often see the negative impact that low self-esteem and lack of confidence in the worth of one's own ideas has on student writing. Barron's call to nurture and foster the student writer's self-confidence as well as skills is urgently needed. It gives educators an opportunity to have students consider the valuable things they have to share and the uniqueness of their voice as part of classroom discussion. To build student confidence and character in writing, teachers need to create meaningful ways for them to experience outstanding examples modeled by known authors to whom students can relate. The work of T. A. Barron meets these criteria.

Figure 3.3 Screenshot of the Barron Prize page on T. A. Barron's web site

EDUCATING STUDENTS FOR LITERATE, INVOLVED CITIZENSHIP

We'd like to draw your attention to the link on Barron's site to the Gloria Barron Prize for Young Heroes (see Figure 3.3), which can be accessed via the Explorations tab. The prize, named for the author's mother, who worked on a museum for children with special needs, "honors outstanding young leaders who have made a significant positive difference to people and our planet. . . . Each year, the Barron Prize selects ten winners nationwide. Half of the winners have focused on helping their communities and fellow beings; half have focused on protecting the health and sustainability of the environment."

What does the prize have to do with inculcating students in the habits of lifelong literacy? To help make the necessary literacy connection between the prize and his own work, Barron has said that he wants everything he writes to promote two ideas: every child has a hero within, and the Earth needs our help in order to conserve, protect, and cherish nature's bounty.

Consider Barron's *The Hero's Trail*. This nonfiction collection of inspiring stories of young people celebrates those who have made a positive difference in their society and also in the environment. How does one connect the book *The Hero's Trail*, which grew out of the endeavor to create the Barron Prize and seems to fit the collected biography/nonfiction genre, to the context of the contemporary accountability and literacy learning mandates with which teachers must cope? Barron has reflected on that issue and has said that he wants his site to encourage young readers to view themselves as positive forces in the world. Young people need help to feel empowered and to feel that they are able to make a positive difference in the world. This is why he has included on his site inspiring stories of real young heroes as well as tales of fictional young heroes from his books.

It's a connecting thematic thread that can be used to tie together Barron's broad range of mythic, adventure, family, social issue, and other relationship-based fiction and nonfiction works. A teacher who is attentive to testing curricula and skills goals can justify teaching and nurturing such citizenship as part of English language arts, social studies, and even science if resources like Barron's site are used to connect all of this content together.

TRY THIS WITH YOUR CLASS

Activity 3.7 I Am a Believer

All grades, all types of learners

T. A. Barron is one of a group of writers who not only create fiction and nonfiction works, but also deliberately embrace a set of values or beliefs that they want to share through their works with their readers.

1. With younger students, share some of Barron's beliefs or the beliefs and values of other authors as stated on their web sites. For example, Jean Craighead George (www.jeancraigheadgeorge.com) feels that taking care of wild life is crucial, and Jane Goodall (www.janegoodall.org) believes in protecting animals from hunting and mistreatment.

2. Model for the students by expressing the beliefs or values (e.g., secular citizenship, whole-child nurturing) that you as an educator bring into the classroom.

3. Ask them what values or important ideas they want to express in their writing and art. Among the ideas the young learners might generate, inspired by Barron or other authors, are respect for every person in the community, caring and helping the elderly and sick, caring for animals, speaking out when others are hurt, making neighborhoods better places by keeping them clean, and helping others less fortunate by donating food, toys, clothes, and service.

4. Once students have come up with a list of their own beliefs, have them place these on the covers or liner pages of their writing notebooks.

5. With older students, ask them to write reflective essays detailing their responses to Barron's beliefs, including the extent to which they share them.

6. As an alternative, ask them to write persuasive essays on the issue of whether an author's work should only reflect certain beliefs and not detail the full spectrum of realities that may contradict those beliefs.

7. Encourage students to share these reflections online with Barron and/or post them in their guest books on other authors' web sites.

Meet the Winners: Enhancing Writing and Discussion Skills

The online gallery of profiles of the winners of the Gloria Barron Prize (www.barronprize .org/winners) is extremely engaging. These are peers ages 8–18 whose community and environmental service achievements are concisely accessible and visible on the site. Ask your students in teams or individually to do the following:

1. Select winners whose picture, age, and location (they are from all over the world) inspires or in some way grabs their immediate attention.

2. Go through the growing gallery of winners, and select at least three whom they can connect with on some level.

3. Prepare a short paragraph explaining how and why they selected these three young heroes.

Specify that in a subsequent class discussion students need to be prepared to describe how their selected heroes are either improving their communities through direct community service or benefiting the planet that we share. Scrolling through the roster of Barron Prize winners, students will find much of interest in the precise, single-paragraph descriptions that incorporate the picture of a young hero in action and are accompanied by at least one comment from the hero about his or her project.

This activity will enhance students' discussion skills, which are difficult and challenging to promote in class, and improve their persuasive writing skills, which always need support. These skills are crucial for success in any number of standardized language arts and social studies tests and often in essay contests, internship/special summer programs, and other special residencies/fellowship opportunities for students.

What's really nice about the Barron Prize site, and developing literacy learning reading and writing workshop lessons around it, is that its topic, like the faces in its gallery of diverse young heroes, is a real one. The Barron Prize's positive purpose of educating for citizenship and constructive action, a term we also use in community service learning at the elementary and secondary levels, is one that connects with students through this gallery of faces similar to their own (see Figure 3.4).

An interesting extension of this activity involves asking students to go through the news, including print and online versions of local newspapers, to identify young heroes who are the same age as the students. Have them use the Winners section of the Barron Prize site as models for authoring their own "Meet Our School or Neighborhood Young Heroes" pieces. Perhaps their efforts can be put on the school or district web site, or maybe students would like to send them to the official Gloria Barron Prize for Young Heroes web site.

To Nominate: Functional and Informational Document Use

Although the site actually requires "thoughtful adults" to submit a nomination, this seeming impediment can be turned to literacy-learning advantage. Have students review the Selection Criteria page (under the Nominate tab), following them carefully to justify in print their nomination of a hero. This critical reading, electronic text, and informational and functional document experience will yield real results. It may well motivate students to complete a nomination package, which is great practice for future scholarship, fellowship, special high school, summer internship, and college admission applications.

Figure 3.4   Screenshot of the Young Heroes Documentary page on T. A. Barron's web site

After going through the nominations process, students decide on an adult they feel comfortable approaching and forward their nomination package to that person. Of course, they will have to convince the adult that their young hero nominee is indeed worthy of this contest. From the learning perspective, they need to demonstrate their critical reading and comprehension of the selection criteria (Document 1) and then share aloud and perhaps in a written paragraph how the young hero that they have selected meets those criteria. They'll need to meet with the adult and get online and to read the To Nominate page together. Since the students are convincing and then hopefully assisting the adult in actually submitting the nomination, they are working on critically reading and communicating information. In other words, they are using the electronic text as a Document 2 that is linked to Document 1, the selection criteria. This body of related skills is required to attain and exceed national, state, and local standards. Students can write sample letters of young hero nomination, revising and perfecting before actually giving it to the adult nominator.

In identifying and nominating a young hero peer for the Barron Prize, students not only engage in authentic writing transactions, but also use oral language skills in reading electronic text. At the end of the process, students will have a strong sense of how they helped another young person get deserved recognition for their efforts.

Extending Learning

Teachers could also incorporate the Barron Prize into an extended literary unit on the theme of heroes and follow the related curriculum that's available for free download on T. A. Barron's site (via the Young Heroes link under the Resources tab). Independent reading could involve students in examining some of the works on heroes suggested in the bibliography of heroes. Of course, they could also make personal use of their sample letters on behalf of the young heroes they identified by entering their comments about these heroes on the My Hero web site (http://myhero.com).

Figure 3.5   Screenshot of T. A. Barron's Special Features page

The Media page of the Barron Prize site is filled with links to provocative and evocative articles and interviews that T. A. Barron has given on the need for students to do community service and improve the planet. This collection of hero-focused news and other nonfiction reader responses connects with Barron's tremendous fascination with heroes, from Merlin to the Tree Girl to the winners of the Barron Prize.

In fact, T. A. Barron celebrates the heroic in nature. His discussion of the glacier lily, a resilient flower that grows high in the Rocky Mountains, is a good example. He notes that this is the first plant to bring the land back to life after an avalanche or storm. In selecting this plant as an emblem of "courage, determination, and hope," Barron, who is also a wilderness educator, makes a wonderful link to science, real-life citizenship and heroism, and literacy.

There is a trove of documents, maps, games, articles, curricula, pictures, audio clips, interviews, media pieces, young hero nomination forms, and testimonials on T. A. Barron's site as well as the Barron Award site. Setting students loose on either one provides them with opportunities to engage in authentic constructive actions, community service, and interactions with adults and peer role models. How much better can teaching and learning be?

ADDITIONAL AUTHOR SITES AND WEB RESOURCES TO EXPLORE

Ursula K. Le Guin

www.ursulakleguin.com/UKL_info.html
This is the official site of the author of *Lavinia, Powers,* and *Gifts,* to name a few of her many titles. One bonus of the site is the many podcasts and recorded interviews with Le Guin. Another is the material available in Spanish. (Grades 4 and up)

Gayle Martin

www.gaylemartinbooks.com/books.html
This is the official site of the author of *Anna's Kitchen, Gunfight at the OK Corral, Billy the Kid,* and other titles. (Grades 3–8)

Katherine Paterson

www.terabithia.com
This is the official site of the author of *The Bridge to Terabitha; The King's Equal; Come Sing, Jimmy Jo;* and other titles. (Grades K–8)

Ralph Fletcher

www.ralphfletcher.com
This is the official site of the author of *The Sandman, Spider Boy, Fig Pudding,* and other titles. Fletcher writes both picture books and chapter books for older students.

David Wisniewski

www.bcplonline.org/kidspage/wisn.html
This deceased, award-winning children's author has no official site, but he is nicely profiled, with bio and a list of his titles, on the Baltimore County Public Library web site. (Grades 3–8)

Edith Nesbit

www.gutenberg.org/browse/authors/n#a407
Nesbit does not have an official site of her own, but readers and teachers can download, for free, *Railway Children* and many of her other titles from the Gutenberg Project. (Grades 4–8)

Fantastic Fiction

http://www.fantasticfiction.co.uk/
For still more sources try this site dedicated to fantasy fiction. It has many resources on other authors who do not have their own sites.

The Spirit of Anne Frank Award

www.annefrank.com/fileadmin/safa/index.html
Information on this award is one of many resources offered on the Anne Frank Center web site.

4

Want to Explore the Components of an Author Site With Judy Blume as Your Guide?

For four decades, the kid-centered, kid-spoken stories of Judy Blume have dominated the world of children's literature. Children as young as six and on up through and their teens have been captivated by such compelling Blume characters as Margaret, Peter Hatcher, Sheila the Great, Fudge, and Sally J. Freedman. The appeal of these characters has pleased several generations of culturally diverse readers, selling over 80 million copies of her children's books, which have been translated into more than 30 languages. Along the way, Blume has earned almost one

Figure 4.1   Screenshot of the home page Judy Blume's web site

hundred distinguished writing awards. She has also written several bestselling books for the adult fiction market.

With close to 30 books in print, clearly Blume has no trouble coming up with ideas for books. But where do these ideas come from? Take the case of *Freckle Juice,* her fourth book, which came out way back in 1971. Judy explains on her web site (www.judyblume .com), "I had a great title, thanks to my daughter Randy, who used to play in the bathtub making a mess with shampoo, soap and powder. She called this concoction freckle juice. All I needed was the story." Blume's books have a memorable flavor because they are often inspired by such bits of real kids' language that she has overheard. Toward the beginning of her career, the children who sourced her ideas were principally her own. In a web site reflection about her moving story *Blubber,* a Blume classic about peer abuse, she shares, "This one is for my kids, who were my experts on 5th grade, bullies, the school bus, and more."

Real-life issues that concern kids deeply are a common thread that runs through many of Blume's books. Her works are compellingly honest renditions of childhood and teen crises that include loss of a parent, divorce, bullying, menstruation, overweight, sibling rivalry, illness, peer scorn, and all sorts of fears—real and imagined. Consequently, her books have deeply touched children and teens throughout the world.

Blume's growing body of children's literature and juvenile trade books are available in foreign language translations in Argentina, the Czech Republic, France, Japan, Korea, Turkey, Serbia, and many other places. While her characters are all American born, the situations, emotions, laughter, tears, and dilemmas they encounter and conquer are universal.

Blume has been a pioneer not only in the frank depiction of issues such as divorce, sexual awakening, and religious dilemma, but also in the use of frank language. Both are aspects of writing traditionally avoided by authors addressing the youth audience. Just as Mark Twain's *Huckleberry Finn* and J. D. Salinger's *Catcher in the Rye* have been among the most challenged works since their publication, so too have Blume's works offended and upset many parents, librarians, school districts, booksellers, and boards of education throughout the United States and abroad. However, this controversy and its accompanying publicity have only increased her sales.

Blume has long recognized that censorship of books and their exclusion from school curricula, libraries, and bookstores not only deprives youngsters the opportunity to read her works, but also discourages the writing of other frank and needed books. Beyond her own popularity and commercial success, Blume worries about other authors whose intended works "will never be written . . . will never be read." Judy notes sadly in the Censorship section of her web site that, "as always, young readers will be the real losers."

Consequently, Blume has become not only a leading and recognized children's trade book author, but also an active and concerned advocate of the First Amendment and a dedicated fighter against censorship. Toward that end, she is part of the Advisory Board for the National Coalition Against Censorship, working to protect intellectual freedom and First Amendments rights. She served as the editor for *Places I Never Meant To Be: Original Stories by Censored Writers* (2001).

Blume has also been a pioneer among the children's and young people's literature community in the use of technology to promote understanding and appreciation of books. She recognized several years ago that her own grandson and his peers, who are also her readers, were consistently to be found online. Just as she always used her stories and characters to reflect young readers' contemporary experiences and lives, she realized that she needed to have an online presence for her readers and teachers beyond her books that were available on the shelves of libraries and bookstores.

EXPLORING THE WEB SITE

Blume's site is a wondrous counterpart to the kid-centered persona she puts forward in her print works. The home page, which says "Welcome to my web site," features a lighthearted and engaging picture of Judy in a kayak.

Along its top border, the site has a navigation bar that links to its various sections, making it easy to see at a glance what is offered and how to get to it (see Figure 4.2). There is a section offering all the important things that young readers want to know about Blume as well as various sections containing the things she wants to share with them.

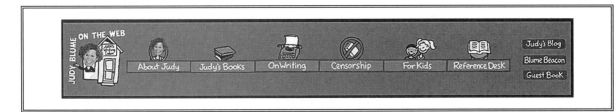

| Figure 4.2 | Screenshot of the navigation bar of Judy Blume's web site |

TRY THIS WITH YOUR CLASS

Activity 4.1 Judy: Likes and Dislikes

Grades 1–3, English Language Learners, Special Needs Readers

1. After visiting Judy Blume's web site with students, challenge them to identify key details about her life (e.g., personality, interests, upcoming projects).

2. List them on an experience chart.

3. Help students use the visual layout of the site to anticipate what Blume's likes and dislikes are.

4. Then have students draw personal Venn diagrams—a highly valuable graphic organizer skill that will prepare them for test taking later on—in which they compare and contrast their interests, likes, and dislikes to Blume's.

About Judy

Moving from left to right on the navigation bar, the first section is titled About Judy. After clicking on it, readers and fans see links to the following sections: Judy's Official Bio, Photo Gallery, How I Became an Author, and Questions for Judy. There are also sections with information for students writing reports about Blume as well as autobiographical essays from the author.

Click on Judy's Official Bio, and you are taken to a personal and professional profile of her life (see Figure 4.3). In four hundred words, the reader moves from Blume's childhood in Elizabeth, New Jersey, through her B.S. in education at New York University, and on to

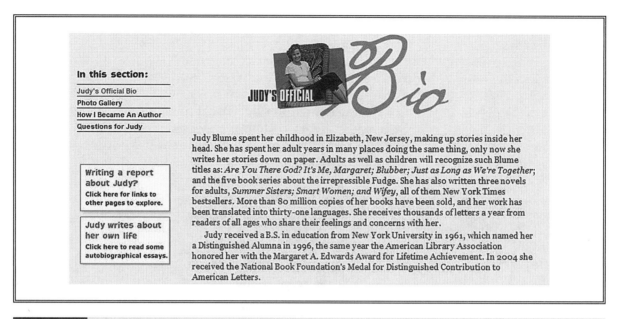

Figure 4.3   Screenshot of Judy Blume's Bio page

her writing many successful books, including *Are You There God? It's Me, Margaret; Blubber; Just as Long as We're Together;* and the five-book Fudge series. The reader follows her involvement with important organizations such as the National Coalition Against Censorship and the Society of Children's Book Writers and Illustrators. Finally, information about her recently and soon-to-be published works is provided.

The Photo Gallery section uses family photos (that are clearly from her real family album) to make Blume come alive for readers, who can connect with the child, mom, and grandmother whose life fed into her literature and is always the core inspiration for her works.

The How I Became an Author section traces Blume's emergence and evolution as an author from her beginnings as a girl who made up stories, but who never dreamed of being a writer. It covers the places she's lived and worked and written about, and relates where she lives now, including a bit about her family and outlook on life.

The Questions for Judy section is arranged in four categories: Personal Things, Family, Writing, and Being a Writer. It includes the questions that all readers and fans want to ask her, such as these:

- What were you like when you were growing up?
- Are any of your other characters based on you or your family?
- How long does it take you to write a book?
- Is it fun to be a writer?

They're all there, anticipating being asked, ready to satisfy and inspire the next generation of writers.

The Judy's Books section of the site lists her works by category: Picture and Storybooks, Pain&Great One Series, The Fudge Books, Middle Grade, Young Adult, and Adult (see Figure 4.4). They are also listed by title. Click on any of the books, and you are whisked to other pages offering a look at the book cover, a short synopsis of the story, a specially selected excerpt from each work, and some great back story insights by Blume herself. She

Figure 4.4   Screenshot of the page listing Judy Blume's books

shares here a little about what moved her to write each book, how she came up with the title, and gives a dedication to the real kids who inspired the characters. This section serves like movie trailers to successfully motivate those who haven't read the books to do so. Even some previous readers of one of Blume's books may be inspired to reread it in light of the author's personal background story. The Judy's Books page also provides a link to a page listing her titles that are available as audiobooks.

TRY THIS WITH YOUR CLASS

Activity 4.2 Excerpt and Book Trailer: Want to Read More About It?

Grades 3–8, Gifted and Talented

1. Use the Judy's Books page for a write-aloud and read-aloud activity. You or your students can read aloud from the excerpts of Blume's books to identify, through class discussion, the components of these successful "trailers." Both visual style and the writing format should be discussed in ways that are grade and age appropriate for the class.

2. Next, challenge students to create print informational and promotional brochures for favorite titles of other authors, to be distributed at the school library or in the children's section of the local public library. If students want, they can use Microsoft Publisher (and other word-processing/desktop publishing software, such as Microsoft Word) to design and mass produce their brochures as part of a schoolwide literacy celebration, or they can upload their material to the class/school web site.

3. To extend the activity, offer students the option of creating 3D promotional book displays, with small squares of the covers of their favorite books off to one side and an opening cutout to include an inviting chapter excerpt.

(Continued)

> (Continued)
>
> 4. With access to a recording device (cassette/tape recorder, digital audio recorder, or audio software), encourage students to read aloud the excerpted chapter and create a recorded teaser, including their own individual appearances as book endorsers. These can be played back in the classroom or school assembly and (if they are in digital format) uploaded to the school or class web site.
>
> Whatever direction this book-description project takes, participant learners get plenty of practice in authentic oral presentation and informational and functional writing.

On Writing

Any teacher and any aspiring young writer will want to tap Blume's personal insights into the writing process. And they'll want to know her feelings and observations about the day-to-day life of a writer as well. To satisfy this, her site's On Writing section opens to a page titled "A Personal View: Judy Talks About Writing" (see Figure 4.5). Here, Blume gives more than a simple "How I got started" or "How I do it." Instead, she isolates and focuses a spotlight on many of the dimensions of her life as a professional writer, giving insight and detail on separate pages, with titles such as Write From the Inside, Your Own Style, Rejection, and The Writing Life. If that weren't enough, Judy's Anxiety Diary gives (what appear to be) real diary excerpts, inside-her-head snapshots that reveal the reality, anxieties included, of this very successful writer. How I Became an Author is the section of author

When I began to write, some people humored me. "You've always been such a dreamer!" Some discouraged me. "Do you know what the odds are...do you know how many would-be writers there are out there?" Some were actually angry. "What makes you think you can write?"

A lot of my readers ask me for "writing tips." I wish it were that easy! There are no hard and fast rules for writing, and no secret tricks, because what works for one person doesn't always work for another. Everybody is different. That's the key to the whole business of writing - your individuality.

I once met a woman who wanted to write. She told me she'd read 72 books about writing but she still couldn't do it. I suggested that instead of reading books about writing, she read the best books she could find, the books that would inspire her to write as well as she could.

On this site, the best I can do is share with you what works for me. Click on one of the topics below (also listed on the left) to read about it, or click here to download a printable version (PDF) of all.

Good luck!

Figure 4.5 Screenshot of Judy Blume's Personal View about writing

sites that all reader-fans want to see. Here, Blume recounts her writer's evolution story in an authentic way that spans a lifetime but that will make sense to and inspire youngsters.

Censorship

As Blume states up front in her bio, she is a longtime advocate of intellectual freedom. It's not surprising, therefore, that another major section of her site—one that educators, librarians, and parents may choose to use—focuses on the topic of censorship. Before one even clicks on the Censorship link, one gets a mouseover message explaining that this section of the web site deals with "what it means, how it affects all of us, what to do about it." Blume deliberately set this page aside to explain her fears about censorship and the ways that, from her perspective, it not only limits and prevents published books from being read and shared, but also deters writers from creating powerful works that may not be published because of their forceful arguments. In this section, Blume informs readers about the existence of censorship, giving insight into why it continues to threaten us, but also provides a collection of informational resources to be explored and examined in depth. These include What to Do If It Happens to You; Is Harry Potter Evil? From the NY Times, 10/22/99; and Judy Blume: A Leader in the Anticensorship Movement, by Mark I. West.

TRY THIS WITH YOUR CLASS

Activity 4.3 Censorship and Me

Grades 4–8

1. Following up on Blume's interest in censorship, have students explore online and in print which of the books they have studied in class or read independently have been challenged. Students generally are surprised by the vast number of books they have already read—titles they either were assigned or discovered on their own—that have come under challenge in some regions of the country.

2. Ask students to summarize the grounds for these books being censored and then write persuasively about the extent to which they feel the grounds were or weren't justified for the particular district, school, or library where the censorship occurred.

3. In a class discussion, help students consider their First Amendment freedoms as well as the potential reasons to curb their right to read.

From our experience, nothing has more motivated students to read a required or suggested text than finding out it was banned or challenged somewhere or removed from bookshelves. The quest to find out the reasons for this challenge, the results of it, and the effect on the sales or popularity of the book are automatic research and critical reading motivators.

For Kids

The For Kids section of Blume's site provides a potpourri of links to segments of interest located throughout the web site (see Figure 4.6). Of particular appeal here is a great trivia quiz about her books, called Did You Know? In this interactive puzzle, kids click on an illustration suggestive of a character or story and find out whether they knew the fact that is revealed.

Figure 4.6 Screenshot of the Kids Page on Judy Blume's web site

TRY THIS WITH YOUR CLASS

Activity 4.4 Fudge Quizzes

Grades 1–3

Children can enjoy interactive quizzes on the Fudge books online at:

http://www.funtrivia.com/trivia-quiz/ForChildren/Double-Fudge-215926.html
http://www.funtrivia.com/trivia-quiz/ForChildren/Superfudge-214195.html
http://www.funtrivia.com/trivia-quiz/ForChildren/Fudge-a-Mania-214261.html

1. Help students use this format to create quizzes for other Judy Blume stories.

2. Have them share their efforts with Blume via her guest book or put them online to check out what peer readers can score.

3. Use student-created quizzes as task cards at the reading center.

4. Involve older students in a read-aloud of something by Blume or another favorite author.

Reference Desk

Clicking on the Reference Desk link will provide visitors to Blume's site with yet more information about Blume, her books, and other related topics (see Figure 4.7). Some of what's to be found here is print; the Autobiographical Essays section houses articles by Blume that are filled with information, facts, and stories about her life. The same is true of

Figure 4.7 Screenshot of the Reference Desk page on Judy Blume's web site

the Audiobooks/DVDs section in which she discusses the recording of her titles that are available as audiobooks. There is also the Judy On the Web section, which is a list of links to various interviews with Blume that can be found online. And there are the More About Judy and More About the Books sections, which are bibliographies of similar items, but without links. For many, though, the Watch and Listen section will be a gem to discover. Here one finds links to online recordings from such sources as National Public Radio, the BBC, and Minnesota Public Radio's Talking Volumes. Click on these to listen to well-produced radio shows featuring interviews with Judy.

Judy's Blog

Over in the right-hand corner of the web site's home page are three not-to-be-missed links to dynamic sections. Blume's blog places her and her readers firmly in the context of Web 2.0 (see Figure 4.8). This frequently updated, informal, stream-of-consciousness record of the things that happen to her, catch her attention, or move her to write a bit about them are set down in the literary spurts that are the hallmark of blogs. Punctuated with still photos and embedded videos, signature media types of the blogosphere, Blume shares her personal and professional life.

Blume Beacon

Directly below the link to the blog is one to The Blume Beacon: A Chronicle of Judy Blume's Most Recent Goings-On! This bulletin of announcements about Blume's books and events (recent and coming up) is put together in the style of a mock newspaper, adding a note of humor. This is something that hardcore Judy Blume fans will want to peruse occasionally.

Figure 4.8   Screenshot of the page header for Judy Blume's blog

Guest Book

And of course, the third part of this triad of links is the Guest Book (see Figure 4.9), which is very real and inviting. Upon landing on this page, one is greeted with a banner stating "Ideas? Suggestions? Something to share? Want to say hi? Just click the 'Add Your Message' button." This section is filled with demonstrations of how Blume's audience establishes a reader's circle of "connected" children, teens, and adults. These comments are posted prominently on the page in an endless scroll that stretches for many dozens of pages, bearing witness to the popularity of her books and the desire of her audience to connect with the author and one another. The posts do not include last names, but do detail ages and personal contexts. Blume's issues and concerns inspire comments not only from children, teens, teachers, librarians, principals, and parents, but also from civil libertarians, book dealers, politicians, first-time writers grappling with censorship, guidance counselors, police, divorce lawyers, school board members, elected officials, and PTA officers.

Figure 4.9   Screenshot of the Guest Book page on Judy Blume's web site

Even without signing the guest book, just in reading the comments, the visitor to Blume's site has a sense of how, on a very regular basis, readers and writers come together to discuss the concerns and issues raised in her works. This is very powerful evidence of a community of readers, writers, and world citizens of all ages.

Because of the volume of comments made, Blume, whose personal and professional calendar is very full, has a trusted assistant read through the guest book, but Blume likes to respond to the most personal messages herself. Urgent requests—for example, librarians defending books or teachers/youth leaders in need of Blume's help in a censorship challenge or school board issue—are likely to get a direct response. Thus, the site serves her mission as an advocate of intellectual freedom. This is a real guest book. And unlike those of some other authors who respond with cloned, one-size-fits-all messages, those who post messages in Blume's guest book know their needs matter to the author, who works hard to stay connected to them.

TRY THIS WITH YOUR CLASS

Activity 4.5 Using the Guest Book and Other Site Features to Get a Sense of an Author's Community of Readers

Grades 3–8

As part of balanced literacy and traditional writers workshop approaches, we often talk about the community of readers and writers. Many students imagine that even a favorite or popular children's author's community includes only children or perhaps teachers and librarians.

1. Suggest that students visit Judy Blume's site (www.judyblume.com) and identify at least four guest book responses that are not from peers or school-affiliated personnel.

2. Ask students to copy down the comments of these individuals and be prepared to share what they learn from this guest book reading about the breadth of the author's audience beyond kids and teachers.

3. For middle school students and gifted/avid reader/researchers, ask them to check a year's worth of an author's guest book entries in order to categorize the range of readership and issues over that time period. Independently or working in small groups, they can chart the author's impact and also identify at least 10–15 particularly interesting comments for discussion.

This activity concretizes the extent to which a powerful and dedicated author exerts an influence that goes way beyond the classroom or school/library community.

Writing a Report About Judy

Back on the Judy's Official Bio page, there is a prominent banner that states "Writing a report about Judy? Click here for links to other pages to explore." Clearly, Blume knows that such an assignment is what sends many young readers to her web site in the first place. And she's obviously eager to help, as this section offers a collection of links to pages throughout the site, which are organized here in a way that turns the site into a research resource, the very thing that such visitors need to accomplish their mission.

TRY THIS WITH YOUR CLASS

Activity 4.6 Checking Out Links for Report Writing

Grades 4–8

Middle grade students who visit Judy Blume's site can click on the "Writing a report about Judy?" link to gather data for a required report on her for an author-study assignment.

1. Challenge students to check out other authors' sites to see if they, too, have labeled links for report writing.

2. If they do, have students download the material and evaluate it.

3. If not, have students collect bio, books, and other information on a given author and send it to that author's site to help their peers.

In so many ways, students visiting Blume's site feel a very special insider connection with her that she has deliberately established. Teachers gain invaluable insights, too, into how to "peg" and motivate the teaching of her works as both stories and life-lesson exemplars.

The anytime accessibility of this web site creates an "author in the house" reality that would otherwise only be possible for the lucky few who get to meet Blume in person. With this site, her devoted readers have a nourishing place to drop into. The door is always open, and the welcome mat is laid out!

A CONVERSATION WITH JUDY BLUME

The Author Talks About Her Web Site

Over a span of more than two decades, I (Rose) have been teaching and sharing Judy Blume's books with my students, Grades 3–12. During that time, I became aware of her activism in the crusade against censorship and her work with the National Coalition Against Censorship (www.ncac.org). At one point I successfully applied for a Judy Blume Kids Fund grant. The money was used to run a successful book banning forum at I.S. 62 in Brooklyn, New York.

While many fashions and fads change in children's literature, their absorption in Judy Blume books has remained a constant over time. Children in my current public school literacy and arts resident programs in East New York and Harlem still connect readily with her works. As I began developing the author site approach, I immediately checked out Blume's site and was delighted to note that it "looked" and sounded very much like the breezy, approachable, engaging Judy Blume. I was able to use the site successfully to inspire many of her younger fans to read even more books by her.

Activity 4.7 Imagine Interviewing the Author

Grades 3–8

Although teachers and adult readers may get a chance to interview authors in person or online, generally students will not have that opportunity. Yet there is usually much biographical and background information on a given author site, which would represent answers to a great many possible interview questions.

1. Before students check out an author site, challenge them, as teams or pairs, to come up with a set of 7–10 questions they would ask the author, were they to have the opportunity.

2. With this list, challenge them to explore the author site and its links to find the author's "answers" to these questions.

3. Have student teams then write their own "unauthorized" but site-researched interviews.

4. Encourage students to enact the interviews, with one student taking the role of the interviewer and the other costumed as the author. The performance can be videotaped and even sent to the author's site.

This interviewing task involves students in close textual study of the author site as a document to align to their own interview-oriented writing. The accuracy of the interview, drawing from on-site evidence, hones document-based question skills, which are important to have in achieving success on a host of standardized English and social studies tests.

When I began writing this book, I immediately contacted Judy Blume. At the time, her site was being redesigned by Mark Tuchman. Judy graciously surprised me with a phone call on April 24, 2006, and the following is a transcript of our conversation.

RR: Your site sounds very much like you; in fact, some other sites are written at a level far beyond the comprehension of their readers and indeed tell their readers not to contact them personally but rather look at the links if they want to learn more. Who does the content and copy on your site?

JB: My concept of an author site is to get to know the author. That's what I want when I visit other author sites, so I decide on the content and write all the copy on mine. That way, the readers, teachers, and librarians who visit my site get to hear from me, not anyone else.

RR: When did you first get the idea to create an author web site?

JB: My husband, George Cooper (a high-tech kind of guy), first suggested we do a web site in the summer of 1996. We sat together for a couple of hours a week tossing around ideas. (I was writing *Summer Sisters* at the time.) I knew only that I wanted the site to be lively, inviting, and true to the spirit of my books. It's evolved over the years to include information about censorship, tips on writing, links to interviews, even video clips—everything I can possibly think of to help students, from elementary schoolers to PhD candidates, find what they need. And, I hope browsers will also find the information interesting.

The site is undergoing a redesign and expansion (I've become so attached to the original, I didn't want to let it go, but George tells me we have to keep it from growing tired.) It will still have the same content and features it has always had. The new designer, Mark Tuchman, will make the site even more interactive and easy to navigate. Mark is very talented, and I'm excited about this collaboration.

Update from Judy: the site is up and running now—all that's missing is the animation on the home page. It's constantly evolving and includes a blog that takes up a lot of time, but I enjoy doing it as it keeps me in touch with my readers.

TRY THIS WITH YOUR CLASS

Activity 4.8 Tweaking an Author Site to Make It Even Better

Grades 6–8, Gifted and Talented

Judy Blume asked Mark Tuchman to update her site to make it even more kid friendly and successful for all visitors. As students become more author-site savvy by being introduced to a growing number of author sites by teachers or exploring them on their own, they will quickly note which sites "rock" and which, while chock full of the standard features, lack things that make them engaging, wonderful experiences, such as pull-and-drag puzzles, movies, media star turns, guest books, and personalized downloadable gifts.

1. Ask students to identify a favorite author site, which like a real home is in need of a serious makeover to encourage even more visitors to the site.

2. Have them review the site and suggest new features, design changes, or updates.

3. Encourage students to send their suggestions to the webmaster or the author.

Who knows? Student makeover artists may receive an e-mail or a letter from a grateful author. Once again, this project provides authentic reader and viewer evaluative response options to an electronic text.

RR: Beyond the fact that your husband, George Cooper, had web expertise, why would you, as a contemporary legend in the children's literature field with massive sales of your print work, feel the necessity of establishing an online author site?

JB: Why not? It's fun. It's today! I love the immediacy, the chance to interact and share with my readers of all ages. If we want kids to read and to communicate, we have to reach them through the technology they're using.

RR: Some writers, librarians, reading specialists, and teacher educators who are very supportive of your books and those of other major authors oppose the use of your site as part of classroom author study. They worry that if students really get involved and enjoy your site, they won't read your print books. They feel that use of author sites may ironically disconnect students from the reading and appreciation of print books. How do you, as a writer who obviously wants students to continue reading your print works, weigh in on this objection to author sites?

JB: I don't agree with this argument, and I'm not worried. I love the idea of teachers using the site with their students—especially after they've shared a book with the class. That's the perfect time to go to the web site to find out more about the book and get a real feel for the author. "Who is the person who wrote this book? Where did the idea come from? Is there more to learn about the characters?" Kids tell me that after visiting my site, they often reread some of my books or check out others they haven't read before.

RR: How do you handle web mail?

JB: I have one trusted assistant who helps me. I try to get back personally to as many readers—kids and adults—as need to hear from me on urgent matters.

RR: As someone who originally connected with you years ago, because of your activism in the battle against censorship, I am eager to have you explain why you, a children's author, include that feature on your site.

JB: Censorship affects all of us. It's important to talk about it. I applaud teachers and librarians who bring the issue to the classroom, who turn it into a lesson about the First Amendment. I believe that the more teachers and librarians talk about censorship issues, the less censorship there will be. Make students aware, and they will be better positioned to defend challenged books.

RR: Has this constructive social action feature of your web site yielded you any proof that it involves your visitors in First Amendment issues?

JB: It certainly has. Librarians, teachers, and students in schools where my books are being challenged will often contact me via my web site. My assistant and I are ready to help in whatever way we can, from sending letters of support to coordinating with various organizations such as the National Coalition Against Censorship, the American Library Association, and the National Council of Teachers of English. It's important for teachers and librarians under fire to know they're not alone in their battles to defend our First Amendment rights.

RR: Thank you so much for your time and your insightful comments.

ADDITIONAL AUTHOR SITES AND WEB RESOURCES TO EXPLORE

The sites listed here parallel Judy Blume's personal writer-to-student tips on the writing process. Using these sites enables you to validate the need for proofing, editing, drafting, and revision, as top bestselling writers explain why they routinely practice these necessary skills.

Everything You Need to Know About Writing Successfully—In Ten Minutes

www.mikeshea.net/Everything_You_Need_to_Kn.html
Stephen King conversationally and succinctly shares revision tips using direct writing examples from his own work. (Grades 4–8)

The Official Frindle Site

http://andrewclements.com/books-frindle.html
This site for author Andrew Clements's master work gives younger readers and middle school students the chance to review the first very short draft of his book *Frindle* (from June 1993) and its second version done later that year. This is a great case study for readers of the work and for middle school students learning how to brainstorm and develop second drafts. (Grades 3–8)

Jane Yolen

www.janeyolen.com

Yolen, who writes across the grade levels (1–8), has very straightforward writing tips on her site. Teachers will especially enjoy the narrative and poetry writing exercises for students. (Grades 3–8)

The Nightmare Room

www.thenightmareroom.com

R. L. Stine provides an unexpectedly rich (and free!) teacher and student resource. His actual journal writing and diary writing editorial markups and enthralling horror genre-specific exercises are perfect for gifted and talented elementary and middle school writers. Since he also provides answers, the activity unit can be used either independently by withholding the answers until students complete the assignments or as part of a class in a horror genre creative writing course. This site is a gem for veteran and new teachers of English language arts, filled with quotes and ideas from a bestselling writer. (Grades 5 and up)

Louis Sachar

www.louissachar.com

This author site has some very good tips on the writing process. (Grades 4–8)

Book Browse

www.bookbrowse.com/author_interviews/list

Check out the interview and two essays by Christopher Paolini, who began his bestselling *Eragon* when he was 15 years old. Of course, the idea that someone in his mid teens was validated with bestselling success already makes any of his tips all the more inspiring to young writers, even though the teacher has stated the same things in class. (Grades 6 and up)

Patricia Polacco

www.patriciapolacco.com

Check out her My Studio feature (by clicking on the Author Info. link and then the A Visit at Work link to get to the My Work section from her home page) for details of how she composes and revises her works. (Grades 3–8)

Ralph Fletcher

www.ralphfletcher.com

Fletcher is a well-known teacher trainer who also writes children's books. His site has succinct student tips for writing and revision. (Grades 6–8)

Banned Books Week Handbook

www.abffe.org

This is a great teaching tool with all one needs to run an event in the classroom.

St. Charles Public Library, Challenged & Banned Books

http://www.st-charles.lib.il.us/arl/arl_banned.htm

Most of these titles are part of most Grade 1–8 curricula or library shelves

5

Illustrators Are Authors, Too!

Drawing pictures is something that fascinates young people universally. For many it is a developmental stepping stone that offers support and satisfaction. In this chapter, we focus on author/illustrators whose books provide a visual feast for young readers while telling wonderful stories about important issues. We explore the world in which these author/illustrators live and work as well as the engaging world they create for their readers. Theirs is a visually riveting world in which the joy and value of books is well established, offering a pathway into the appreciation of written language for students who might not get there otherwise. We are welcomed into this world via their web sites.

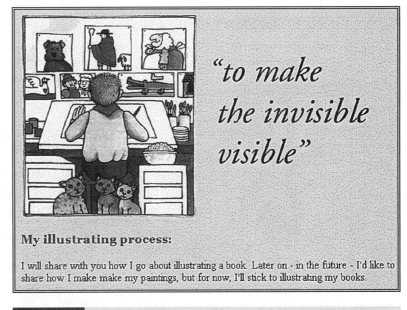

"to make the invisible visible"

My illustrating process:

I will share with you how I go about illustrating a book. Later on - in the future - I'd like to share how I make make my paintings, but for now, I'll stick to illustrating my books.

Figure 5.1 Screenshot from Tomie dePaola's web site

Just as the authors in the previous chapters share insights into the process of writing and being a writer, in this chapter Chris Van Allsburg, Kevin Henkes, and Tomie dePaola share what it is like to be an artist, how they make their wonderful pictures, and what the life of an author/illustrator is like. In a sense, these visually oriented authors parallel the others highlighted in this book in making students their learning apprentices. Kids for whom art is a lifeline are given an opportunity to be thoroughly engaged in the world of books by having their interest in making art married to the world of literature. They are also offered compelling discussions and demonstrations of techniques and approaches taken by favored author/illustrators. In the process, they are exposed to role models with whom they can strongly identify.

A good example of how this apprenticeship is fostered can be seen in the screenshot from Tomie dePaola's web site shown in Figure 5.1, a site that very effectively combines the creative processes of writing and illustrating. A stylized version of the artist is shown at his drafting table, with illustrations from some of his best-known books on the wall in front of him. Children are invited in, not only by the warm colors, the familiar illustrations, and the kittens who sit by the artist's stool, but by the fact that in this drawing, the artist himself— seen from the back—looks like a child. The artist has made the invisible visible, conveying the joy of illustration through the drawing itself.

THE CHALLENGE FOR CERTAIN LEARNERS TO ENGAGE WITH AUTHOR TEXTS

There are likely a number of factors that account for certain students' lack of engagement with books and authors. For each of them there may be a unique reason why words alone don't draw him or her in. However, there are some general reasons why not all learners engage immediately.

Visual and Spatial Learners

Some students are terrific at observation. They continually make small drawings on pages that are meant to be filled with words. They may hand in regular word sheets or work

Figure 5.2   The entry point to Chris Van Allsburg's web site

pages with doodles on the edges or back that show real artistic expressiveness. But when what's required is a sentence or paragraph response or a correct single word or phrase, drawings are not accepted as a substitute.

TRY THIS WITH YOUR CLASS

Activity 5.1 Image or Story: What Comes First?

All Grades, including English Language Learners

1. Have students think about the way an author/illustrator whose work you are studying in class creates his books.

2. Ask them what they think comes first, the pictures or the story.

3. Discuss this as a group, making reference to book covers or other illustrations that you know students will find on the author/illustrator's web site.

4. Let them write down their ideas, if appropriate.

5. Next, have students independently explore the web site(s), discover and reflect on the illustrations they find, and share their findings.

This activity will thoroughly engage students in worthwhile writing activities as well as deepen their connection to books. It makes them part of the ongoing process of reading, reflecting, responding, and sharing about what they read.

Many students are visual learners and can't bridge that visual capacity to cross over into the necessary linguistic realm. They are challenged to respond in words to questions about content. Their parents may be comforted with assurances that these youngsters may handle themselves great in the real world of designing, engineering, or a wide variety of other creative outlets, even though they are challenged by the mandated, text-based reports, projects, and tests commonly assigned in school.

This is one of the great problems today with standardized tests and the instructional culture that has formed around them. Unfortunately, in the No Child Left Behind climate of testing and teacher accountability, visual learners are largely left out, with little to encourage them to fully embrace a love of reading and writing, and are prevented from demonstrating their actual abilities on standardized tests that are basically word driven. This key issue has long been a concern to teachers, but is now even more so.

English Language Learners

Today, classes in the United States have increasing numbers of English Language Learners (ELLs). This is of concern to more than just those teachers officially designated as teachers of ELLs. It is common for ELLs to spend part of their time in classes not well suited for their needs. These students are often taught the same curriculum that is mandated for mainstream students at their age or grade level. Many of them achieve to that grade level, but because the English language is either not their first language or is not spoken at home, they are literally not taken by the power of the written and spoken English word; some of the natural lure of the word for them is diminished.

TRY THIS WITH YOUR CLASS

Activity 5.2 Creating Illustrated Story Book Covers

Grades 3–8

The relationship between story and picture is a rich area to explore as part of the process of creating meaning. Of the numerous pictures that author/illustrators generate for a full book, the cover illustration is the most important. It represents the meaning and emotional content of the book in its entirety. To get greater understanding of cover illustrations, have students visit and review the content of author web sites, such as that of Gail Gibbons (www.gailgibbons.com), which has a page of nothing but covers.

1. Have students reflect on the cover illustration of a book you are about to begin work on. Ask them what they expect to experience from it based on the cover.

2. Repeat this process at the conclusion of work on that book, asking how well the cover illustration represented the book.

3. Have students select a story for which they will design the all-important cover illustration. For convenience, a classic children's story such as Puss 'n Boots or Hansel and Gretel will suffice, although many other types of stories can be adapted to this activity. If you have many students from multicultural backgrounds who do not know these stories, substitute a storybook they have read as a class or have them make a story book about their family.

4. After students draw their cover illustrations, assemble a class display and have students present and explain their decisions to their peers.

Easy technology extension: Scan the finished cover illustrations, saving them as JPG files (standard digital photo format). These can then be uploaded easily to any of the free photo sharing web sites (e.g., Picasa, http://picasa.google.com; Flikr, www.flickr.com; Photobucket, http://photobucket.com), where a class gallery can be easily established. Many of these resources allow for captions and small amounts of text to be added, enabling students to convey more meaning (see also Chapter 6).

The Unique Powers of Illustrator Sites

We have explored the work of Eric Carle already, but there are many more key children's authors who are also professionally trained illustrators and artists. These are authors featured in school and classroom libraries whose books are often arts inspired and who celebrate art as an entry point for their writing. Some excellent examples are Chris Van Allsburg, Kevin Henkes, Tomie dePaola, and Allen Say.

Van Allsburg's work, which has some dark nuances and mysteries, is excellent for older students up to Grades 6–8. Say produces wonderful material that deals with cultural differences and historical research appropriate for a broad range of students, but some of his work is definitely better for junior high students. Henkes and dePaola generally write for the younger grades, but Henkes did write *Olive's Ocean* for middle school audiences and ELLs will really appreciate the simplicity and straightforward nature of dePaola's work, even if they are in middle grades.

How do these author/ illustrators draw readers in through their web sites?

| Figure 5.3 | Screenshot of Chris Van Allsburg's home page |

CHRIS VAN ALLSBURG

The Illustrator as Designer of a Captivating State-of-the-Art Site

To answer this question, simply type in www.chrisvanallsburg.com and literally enter the world of Chris Van Allsburg (see Figure 5.2 on page 70). His home page (see Figure 5.3) will catch the attention of visual learners, and likely, its draw is emotional, a dimension that's not a part of English language learning as currently taught in our schools.

The home page very much reads like any other standard author site, and Van Allsburg explains the reason for the site in his Message From Chris: "Unfortunately, reading is about all I can do with the many letters I receive. I just don't have enough time to answer each and every one. And so, with a little help from some friends, I have created this website to help answer your questions and to share with you a little bit more of my work."

By clicking around the home page and exploring the site, you can model for students how to navigate so that they can later explore for themselves. The interactive link signals the sections of the site where students can provide their own input, making the site truly learner centered.

Puzzles Push, Pull, and Drag Site Visitors Into Literacy

After clicking on the games link on the interactive page, there are terrific activities to be found: click-and-drag puzzles, shuffle puzzles, and memory games. These just may

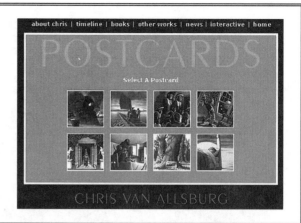

Figure 5.4 Screenshots of the Drawings and Postcards sections of Chris Van Allsburg's web site

literally drag students into engaging with the text. As Ali, an elementary school teacher, explains:

> This web site is magnificent for students who are visual learners, auditory learners, and for learners who enjoy solving puzzles. Students who use their memory skills in the web site, while playing the visual memory game. The younger students can use the puzzles to match specific objects with the correct object. . . . Older students can use the interactive puzzles to shuffle the pieces to complete the picture in perfect order.
>
> For those students who are linguistic and visually inclined, the scavenger hunt with its point rewards is a wonderful way to target and assess students' comprehension of the site through a quiz that also is student directed and visually motivating.
>
> Another aspect of this site that only a genuine author/illustrator would use concerns the book list. A great many author sites include a list of books published by the author, but Van Allsburg's site also allows visitors to not only click on the book descriptions, but also to click on the actual book covers.
>
> Another great area of Van Allsburg's site to explore is the Coloring page in the Interactive section. Student artists, ELLs, and shy students who don't speak in class can use tools online to simulate the style and color range of the very distinctive Van Allsburg palette. This allows for collaborative illustration/authoring, which is a greatly extended version of the traditional author prompts given to student writers that are offered by other author sites as invitations to interactive exercises.

TRY THIS WITH YOUR CLASS

Activity 5.3 Illustration Jigsaw Puzzles

Grades K–3, Students With Special Needs

Many sites include coloring pages and puzzles derived from illustrations from the authors' key books. These extras provide the opportunity to involve students in the world an author creates—enhancing, enriching, and extending the books.

1. Have students download and then print out favorite or key teaching illustrations (or do this for them).

2. Attach the downloaded image to poster board/cardboard, and divide it into random jigsaw-shaped pieces to create a puzzle for students to put together (fewer pieces for lower-level students, more for higher-level, etc.).

Now that students are drawn into the author's virtual world and are collaborating with Van Allsburg on finishing a work of art, you can ask them to explain why they made specific color decisions. This explanation can be either written or oral, and afterward can become a focus for discussion among the students.

Van Allsburg Shares His Experience

There's a great deal of literacy-related art as entry-point material on this site. In the Interactive section, the Video Clips has short videos that present Van Allsburg talking about his experiences in art school and his unconventional approach to entering his field. This approach validates and affirms art as an entry point for writing. It uses all the rich video, interactive, multisensory powers of the web to convince and validate the artist as a potentially powerful writer. Students will love the channel-changing navigational device for learning about the videos and selecting which ones to watch.

Overall Value of the Web Site

Just as visual learners may be drawn into the overall book experience through this entry point, other types of learners may be attracted by the broad range of items and activities offered. Some may follow Fritz the dog on a great text-driven scavenger hunt. Other independent learners can listen to Van Allsburg's speeches. All can check out the virtual exhibits of his sculptures, posters, and sketches, finding much to inspire, motivate, and direct them in their growth as readers and writers (see Figure 5.4).

This extraordinary site, with its high-tech, rich, arts-driven opportunities and options should draw in visual learners and ELLs, as well as kinesthetic learners who won't be able to resist the puzzles, videos, and the other dynamic aspects of the experience that the site offers. Focusing on author/illustrators can expand the appeal of and draw slow-to-participate students into the classroom's circle of readers and writers. Van Allsburg's web site makes a compelling case for the use of illustrator sites to promote literacy.

TRY THIS WITH YOUR CLASS

Activity 5.4 Author Dream Sites: Reflecting on Author Web Site Features

Grades 6–8

1. Have students brainstorm a list of author/illustrators they are familiar with.

2. From this list, assign each student an author to investigate on the web. It is fine to have several students work on the same author or perhaps, depending on the number of students involved and the number of computers available, have them work as small teams.

(Continued)

(Continued)

3. Instruct students to conduct a review of their assigned site, listing the features they find there.

4. Have each report back to the class on one or two of the most interesting features they find that they feel add value to the web site. Challenge them to explain how the features they select add to their experience of the author's work.

5. Finally, after the whole-class sharing activity, ask students to select one feature that they feel their favorite author's site should include but doesn't. Have them write a short passage explaining this decision.

TRY THIS WITH YOUR CLASS

Activity 5.5 Author Site Souvenir Postcards

All Grades, Including Students With Special Needs and English Language Learners

1. Challenge students to create postcard designs that can be a souvenir of having visited a favorite author's web site. These postcards would feature quotes taken from the author's books and student-drawn illustrations based on the author's graphic style.

2. Direct students to begin with either a quote or an image reminiscent of a chosen book. The image can be drawn on 5" x 7" paper or card stock and the quote produced on a word processor and then cut and pasted next to the image.

Easy technology extension: After the postcard's image has been drawn, scan it and save it as a JPG file (standard digital photo format). Next, import the file into Microsoft Word (or another word-processing program), and type the quote directly in the same space as the graphic using the Text Box feature. The final postcard can be printed out with a conventional printer, yielding a professional looking card.

The pairing of key phrases and statements from a book's text with iconic, easily recognizable images that make strong reference to the characters, places, and happenings of the book will make for a highly meaningful experience for students and teachers.

Tech Needs?

Sites like that of Chris Van Allsburg are designed to run on any relatively recently manufactured computer with a broadband Internet connection. The latest, most powerful and elaborate machines are not a requirement! Clearly, it wouldn't do the author, who is very focused on expanding his audience, any good if only teachers with the most well-endowed technology resources could take advantage of it.

Use of these sites could be adopted as a standard by which schools and districts can measure the viability of the technology provided to general classroom teachers. Is your technology up to this modest set of requirements? You might confer with your school or district tech coordinator, who should be able to advise appropriately. Better yet, why not just try it? Go to a web site such as Van Allsburg's, and see what happens. If, on the outside chance, your school's technology is too rudimentary to support the modest requirements of such a site, then the site's features simply won't run well. It's is a simple, no-risk test.

For those who don't have access to even this minimum level of technology, there are still ways to take advantage of the approach presented here, even if all of the resources cited can't be used. Further, there are illustrator sites that can be accessed on even what many today would consider to be outdated computers. One such site as that of Kevin Henkes, whom we visit next.

KEVIN HENKES

Child-Friendly Fun and Games, With Downloadable Coloring Pages

Teachers can use the work of the 2005 Caldecott medal winner Kevin Henkes for a broad spectrum of achievers in fourth or fifth grade. His rich novels have lots of authentic themes and topics that are relevant to students' lives: tolerance, conflict resolution, death. His picture books have characters who demonstrate key values in life: reliability, resilience, bravery, and smarts—all qualities we want students to emulate. His Mouse Books are probably the most famous.

Henkes's web site is a great resource for drawing in students who don't exactly love the printed word. Various elements of the site can be used to differentiate instruction and to accommodate different learning styles.

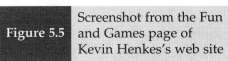

Figure 5.5 Screenshot from the Fun and Games page of Kevin Henkes's web site

Click and Interact With Characters and Illustrations

Henkes's site (www.kevinhenkes.com) is well formatted and has many links. The colorful and popular Mouse Books section allows students to learn about not only each book in the series, but also the individual characters. Students can click on the picture icons and use them as entry points for talking about what each of these character's values are.

The delightful activities on the Fun and Games page of the Mouse Book section can be used to implement a character development comprehension focus. Children would enjoy the offerings on this page, which would also help them feel even more of a bonding connection to the characters. The Celebrate Lilly's Big Day feature (see Figure 5.5) includes a great picture matching game, which provides a kinesthetic and spatial entry point for ELLs and visual learners. (It may require Adobe's free, downloadable Acrobat Reader.)

Even advanced elementary learners get a tremendous kick out of printing the coloring pages on the Fun and Games page, with their illustrations of Lilly at her desk and Lilly with her purple purse. By printing these pages, looking at the where Henkes has actually placed his drawing, and coloring the pages, students literally "color" a connection to a circle of illustrators and authors. Every student, not only the advanced or on-grade-level vocabulary users, can access that circle and both literally and metaphorically make literacy links through these online features.

The Fun and Games section has a wonderful coloring sheet called Everyone Can Be an Artist, which is a great way to draw student artists into the circle of readers and writers. The art generated by students who are spatial/visual learners can be used to prompt their work on stories. This will really get those students into the lifelong habit of constructing meaning, which is so much a part of reading through writing and the balanced literacy writing workshop. Yet linguistic learners are not left behind in the Fun and Games here, since the character games also include the tried-and-true standard word searches and some great procedural accounts-based exercises.

⭐ **Refreshments:**

Every party needs snacks. Ask an adult to help you make these recipes!

Mr Slinger's Zinger Punch

Two 10-ounce packages frozen sweetened strawberries
One 6-ounce can frozen lemonade concentrate
1/4 cup sugar
Two 28-ounce bottles chilled ginger ale
One 28-ounce bottle chilled club soda

In a covered blender at high speed, blend strawberries, undiluted lemonade concentrate, and sugar until thoroughly blended. Pour mixture into a large punch bowl and add remaining ingredients. If your mouse guests like things really chilly, add ice.

Figure 5.6 Screenshot of a recipe from the Fun and Games section of Kevin Henkes's web site

Using Procedural Account Recipes to Practice Test-Taking Skills

To teach procedural accounts, use this site's recipes for Mr. Slinger's Zinger Punch (see Figure 5.6), Chester's Peanut Butter Toasties, and Lilly's Luscious Cheese Bites, all of which can be found on the Fun and Games page. These recipes connected with the characters' favorite snacks make a tactile/kinesthetic and (potentially) mathematics/literacy connection for learners of various types. Plus, they simply make Henkes and his characters come alive for young readers who probably share one or more of the character's tastes in snacking.

Literacy coaches and test-sophistication consultants would agree that these recipes have multiple uses beyond promoting peanut butter, cream cheese, and lemonade consumption. They can be used as model documents to help acclimate young and middle school readers to nonfiction excerpts that can appear on standardized reading tests and document-based questioning multiple-choice standardized reading and mathematics tests.

You can use this part of the Fun and Games section of Henkes's site for necessary practice of test sophistication skills for both mathematics problem solving and measurement and procedural account sequencing. A side benefit is the edible product that a class can make as a group activity or that learners can make at home.

TRY THIS WITH YOUR CLASS

Activity 5.6 Understanding Authors' Values

All Grades, Including Students With Special Needs and English Language Learners

1. Have students explore the images on an author's site, especially in the biography section, and identify at least two to three that demonstrate what they believe are values that are important to the author.

2. Challenge them to explain in a short essay how the images communicate this.

3. Have them follow up with an oral presentation to the class, supported by projecting the selected images with an LCD for class peers to see.

Figure 5.7 Screenshot of the Mouse Books page on Kevin Henkes's web site

Previewing Books for All Ages Online

Henkes has written several novels, which students can learn about on his site. The plots are briefly described on the *more novels* page, allowing students to browse before any further investigation. Each book description also contains a link that takes students a level deeper, where they can read a chapter excerpt of appreciable length. This feature allows them to decide whether they are interested in the story. If so, they would probably be motivated to read the book. It also nicely models the style of the bookseller web sites (e.g., Borders, Amazon), which often offer the reader/book purchaser the opportunity to read an excerpt of the book online before purchasing it. Independent readers or even small groups of students might explore this feature and, during the sharing portion of reading or writing workshop lessons, provide previews and synopses of the plots of each of the novels.

As we have pointed out, many upper elementary classes these days have a vast range of students, including visual learners and ELLs. Teachers of such classes might want to offer these students the possibility of previewing the text of the Picture Books or Mouse Books link. Also, mainstream students can be asked to review the books for ELLs who are new to the United States or for younger peers or siblings in first or second grade. With positive memories or associations with Henkes's famous characters, every student will love having the opportunity to investigate something in order to share it with younger kids. This puts them on a teacher/mentor literacy level with regard to another child, which is a great reader self-concept builder for students who are not yet on appropriate grade and reading levels for their chronological ages.

TRY THIS WITH YOUR CLASS

Activity 5.7 Shifting Story Settings

All Grades

While working with an author/illustrator's book in class, focus on the story's setting (e.g., time frame, country or geographical location, culture).

1. Have students choose an alternative setting and research it with an eye toward redoing the book. Challenge them to shift the setting by changing the costumes and other cultural artifacts illustrated in the book so that they fit another region or time period.

2. Discuss these questions with students: Which things could and could not be shifted? Which were easy or difficult to shift, and why?

3. Going beyond the research, reflection, and discussion, have students select a passage and an illustration or two to redo, producing a finished piece to look as if it were done by the author/illustrator.

The Author/Illustrator Talks About His Work

The Picture Books section of this very accessible web site offers a conversational Story Behind the Book for Henkes's award winning *Kitten's First Full Moon*. In fact, the design of this section nicely follows the visual layout of his printed work, which he explains to the reader/visitor to his online "home":

From the very beginning I pictured the book with black-and-white illustrations, bold sans serif type, a square trim size, and soft, creamy paper. I love to use color—even bright color—in most of my picture books, but for this book color seemed unnecessary. I thought that by keeping everything as simple and spare as possible, a better, tighter, more complete book would result. I liked the idea of having a white moon, a white cat, and a white bowl of milk surrounded by the black night.

His explanation is a wonderful, visually oriented prompt for individual or perhaps small-group collaborative storytelling, writing, and illustrating activities. The fact that it is given by the author as he visits the classroom, courtesy of the site tour, is perfect.

Henkes's discussion of how he drew with a brush and did his art in tribute to Claire Turley Newberry's illustrations of cats will also prove highly engaging to young artists and/or visual learners. This is a great example of how this author/illustrator's site uses illustration as the hook for drawing artists/readers in to his dynamic literacy circle. It can be shared with both younger and older students.

Students who spend every spare minute drawing (including those minutes that are not spare and are supposed to be spent doing reading and writing tasks) will be drawn into Henkes's biography section by his opening line: "I remember drawing at a very early age. I loved it. And my parents and teachers told me I was good at it—that made me love it all the more."

TRY THIS WITH YOUR CLASS

Activity 5.8 Analyzing the Storybook Kitchen

Grades 2–5

Challenge students to do an imaginary review of the foods that are written about in an author/illustrator's books. Their review may include a restaurant critic–type response to the taste and presentation of the foods and an analysis of the recipe, ingredients, and procedures and practicalities of cooking them.

There is also an enlightening interview with Henkes on his site. It contains responses that only an author/illustrator would make to the classic questions about a writer's life. Here are a few of his comments that teachers can use as prompts for student reflections:

I grew up desperately wanting to be an artist. That desire was a huge part of my identity for as far back as I can remember.

I often edit as I write, knowing that the pictures will provide important information. For example, in *Chester's Way,* I didn't mention Lilly's boots, crown, or cape when I wrote the story, although I knew long before the manuscript was finished that Lilly would be wearing them.

[On writing novels versus picture books] Because I'm a visual person, I do have very strong images in my head as I work. I love describing my characters and their environments. Setting a scene—providing proper lighting, the colors and textures of things, sounds—is one of my favorite things about writing a novel.

This interview offers rich potential for independent or guided reading for advanced fourth graders and middle school students who can see, hear, and truly connect with Henkes on visual and interactive levels. It provides a feeling very similar to being guided by an expert through an exhibit of an artist's work or walking around with a recorded gallery guide. Only, in this tour, Henkes himself is available to guide us through the art with his own personal commentary.

Perhaps the only flaw to this site has to do with getting in touch with Henkes. Unlike the sites of most young people's authors, apart from registering to receive his online newsletter periodically, there is no way to contact him or get a response from him.

TRY THIS WITH YOUR CLASS

Activity 5.9 Animal Studies

Grades 3–8

Animal-based characters that appear in studied author/illustrators' books can be the basis for a brief research activity. Have students determine the extent to which illustrator-depicted animals reflect real animal characteristics.

This activity provides a nice nonfiction connection to the work of fictional animals in author/illustrators' works. In researching and developing a nonfiction connection/knowledge base for the fictional animal character, students work with two documents: the fictional animal narrative and the nonfiction report they research. This provides practice in exactly the document-based essay and comparison skills needed for success on many elementary and middle school standardized tests.

TOMIE DEPAOLA

Warm and Fuzzy Web Site, Up Close and Personal

Tomie dePaola

(pronounced Tommy da-POW-la) is best known for his books for children.

He's been published for 40 years and has written and/or illustrated over 200 books, including *26 Fairmount Avenue*, *Strega Nona*, and *Meet the Barkers*.

Tomie dePaola and his work have been recognized with the Caldecott Honor Award, the Newbery Honor Award and the New Hampshire Governor's Arts Award of Living Treasure.

He lives in New London, New Hampshire with his new Airedale dog, Brontë.

1999 ©SUKI COUGHLIN/PAULA MCFARLAND, STYLIST

Figure 5.8 Screenshot from the About Tomie page on Tomie dePaola's web site

Now let's look at Tomie dePaola's web site (www.tomie.com). Staring out at us from the About Tomie page is a terrific photo of Tomie with his paintbrushes, fully demonstrating his identity as an artist (see Figure 5.8). Let's check out the links on the left-hand side of his site. Note the simple noncluttered style of his links, very few and all to the point, an approach that makes them highly inviting to students. Those who have read or heard his works read aloud will recognize the heart design that is his signature art from his books.

TRY THIS WITH YOUR CLASS

Activity 5.10 Portrait of the Illustrator

Grades 6–8

Have students use different sources to get a balanced view of an illustrator. One source should be the official biography from the About Me or Bio section of the illustrator's web site. Other information can be gleaned from the wide variety of material available about many authors on the web, material posted by reviewers, biographers, or collaborating authors or artists. Have students report on information provided by any unofficial sites as well as the official site, and compare and contrast the understanding of the author that emerges from both—good for document-based questioning and critical-analysis test practice.

DePaola's web site appears deceptively unsophisticated and perhaps not as initially mesmerizing to young readers as that of, say, Chris Van Allsburg, but in its subtle way it is very thorough and effective. Bigger and more multimedia-enriched effects are not always a better or appropriate approach to a web site for a given writer, which is an excellent principle for young readers and educators alike to understand. As we introduce students to web resources, it is useful to contextualize the activity with the metaphor of going to visit the author at his home site (emphasis on "home") and, as we suggested for Eric Carle's site, have them anticipate what that home site will be like.

Author site design and development should be focused on reflecting the particular author's skill and style of writing (and illustrating, in the case of the authors highlighted in this chapter) and being appropriate for both teachers and students, plus the parent audience the author addresses. Some authors have a vast range of audiences of different ages, so their site design often features different sections that are appropriate for those different audiences. For example, dePaola's site has bibliographic data that teachers can use to find further information on the web about dePaola, his awards, autobiographical stories, and appearances.

In the About Tomie section, dePaola shares great pictures of him and his Airedale dog Brontë. These will interest kids, as will the details in his FAQs about his dancing, which reveals another layer to his personality.

An author site should have materials that are perhaps a bit above students' comprehension level, but that can be used to inspire students to read the author's work or to affirm for students that their unique talents—as in the case of the illustrators—are part and parcel of the writing and literacy exercises, the stuff of daily instruction. dePaola's site includes coloring pages that are available for downloading and a calendar with key dates and birthdays of his family and friends, as well as references to history, culture, and characters from dePaola's books. Using the calendar and the coloring pages can connect students who need arts-based introductions to the English language or initial literacy experiences to dePaola.

Being an Artist

With an identity firmly rooted in being an artist, it is not surprising that dePaola has a section on his site titled Being an Artist. He uses this section as a kind of insider's view of his process of authoring and illustrating (see Figure 5.9). Certainly, though, it could also be read aloud as part of a literacy lesson. dePaola's process of both writing and illustrating is very focused on revision. This, of course, is what the writing process is all about.

In terms of getting authentic insider information and a slew of resources for differentiated instruction to engage a broad spectrum of learners (including special needs, ELL, gifted and talented, and, for the purpose of this discussion, young artists), this site is a treasure trove. And the Being an Artist section is the jewel in the crown.

This section is chock full of dePaola's autobiographical memories of growing up Irish and Catholic. It has great insider stuff, including a back story on Flossie (his mom) and the house on 26 Fairmount Avenue, on which he's based a series of books. The archived Tomie Says pieces provide wonderful insights into Mrs. Bowers, his own teacher who inspired *The Art Lesson,* and lots of other stuff that dePaola's readers can research and present.

Memoirs and Reviews

The site's People Say section (under About Tomie) is essentially a collection of his friends' memory snapshots of dePaola as a person, as a struggling but dance-loving young artist. This material can be used for minilessons and for independent learners to explore and share with the whole class.

This section may seem too deep for students in Grades 4–6 and certainly for most of dePaola's young readers. However, you can facilitate this material for students by reading aloud some of the selections and giving students lots of opportunities to discuss them as part of guided or shared read-aloud lessons. They can also be used in write-aloud minilessons to model for students the genre of the reminiscence or snapshot memoir. These friends' stories of dePaola at different periods in his life share an aspect of his personality that will interest students. One gets a glimpse of him as a young, slim, nervous schoolboy from the description that Bernice Hunt (aka Lisa Miller) gives in her "My Young Friend" selection. She shares how he made gorgeous dinners for her, went disco dancing, and liked the Beatles and singers in supper clubs. Other highlights can excite and inspire children, including the cover of the first early childhood science book that dePaola illustrated and the insights of another author, Barbra Elleman, who wrote the book *Tomie dePaola: His Art and His Stories.*

Certainly, this section of the web site alone justifies visiting it and using it to enrich minilessons and differentiated instruction. But how can this stuff be directly used by students who will perhaps explore the site as independent readers and writers? Of course, they would have to be reading on or above grade level to comprehend it. But how could such Grade 4–6 students even begin to appreciate the potential in this material on their own?

They would need the teacher to give them a prompt or ask them perhaps to be ready to portray these various friends of dePaola's, sharing their memories of him aloud. Students could also be asked to make a connection by sharing their own memories as stories of specific events or holidays or dinners with a cherished friend or family member. They might even be assigned a project in which they interview and get memory stories about a commonly known friend from many individuals who know the person. Keeping the connection to dePaola's web site, they could then create a "People Say" scrapbook or even a web site. Such a project would help students learn to deal with timelines, citizenship education, memoir writing, production of a text-based product, and web design.

Teachers can also use some of the pieces in this collection on dePaola's site to introduce students, particularly those who are advanced readers and writers in Grades 4–6, to the genre of literary criticism—writing about a writer's work. Students in Grades 4 and above are accustomed to doing reports, so the notion of the obligatory report on a particular country or person or history event is a familiar one to them. These works in the People Say section show that writers and their writings can be the subject of reports that others take pleasure in reading. In particular, Barbara Elleman's piece introduces that aspect of literary criticism. Why not use this piece and others here as starting points for having interested young readers start reading some of the online reports, reviews, and analyses of their favorite or featured class authors that are available for their immediate reading? Who says that these reviews and bits of literary criticism that authors include on their sites are just for teachers?

Certainly, author sites and their collected bibliographical links provide teachers with tremendous resources for serving the needs of an underserved segment of the student population: gifted, talented, and/or accelerated learners who are often left to their own devices and have already developed subject and theme interests. Why not let them be exposed to some "adult" advanced writing genre and see what types of in-the-style-of models they can develop or present?

Figure 5.9 Screenshots from the "Spotlight On. . ." (Strega Nona) page on Tomie dePaola's web site

Note: The figure on the right shows rough sketches, giving insight into the artist's process behind the finished books.

ALLEN SAY

Now let's take a look at the author/illustrator Allen Say, whose work covers a vast spectrum of key social studies and language arts topics and themes. For instance, there is the wonderful *Grandfather's Journey*, a book on the subject of immigration and a great resource for social studies units on that theme. There's also *The Lost Lake*, which has simply magnificent illustrations of the natural world that can go with any science content in Grades 5 and above, making nature real for students.

Unlike so many authors and illustrators who have authorized sites, Say has not offered one to his readers yet. This is unfortunate because many educators routinely use his works because they are so perfect for instructional units on Asia, immigration, and multicultural understanding. However, Say's publisher, Houghton Mifflin, has created a publisher's site for him with a lot of data (http://www.houghtonmifflinbooks.com/authors/allensay). Educators can make good use of publishers' sites if authors don't establish authorized sites on their own. When I (Rose) questioned Say about why he didn't have an official site, he stated that he hated the concept of establishing his own author site, but he was aware that his publisher had put one up for him. The fact that the occasional author, like Say, doesn't see the same potential and importance in authors' sites that the vast majority do offers a good opportunity to involve students in a writing activity. Assign students who have already done some author site reviews the task of persuading siteless authors like Say to establish one. This would make a valid and authentic business and persuasive letter-writing activity.

FROM SITE CONSUMER TO SITE CREATOR

Beyond writing about the value of an author web site, students can go through the exercise of planning one for an author of interest. Students who have reviewed at least three author sites would recognize the key components shared by most of them. Additionally, they have a good idea about what games, activities, and sections would best suit an author whose work they have studied. Without getting too deeply involved in the technology of web sites, perhaps using a simple word-processing document or publisher, students can plan and "rough out" a home page and a few subsidiary linked pages to suit an author of their choice. In fact, current versions of word-processing programs, such as Microsoft Word, allow for the creation of hyperlinks within a single document, and a bit of the experience of a live web site can be approximated in this way.

The real point of this exercise, however, is to plan a site, not execute it. Based on what's been inferred by visiting and analyzing real author sites, which sections, functions, and features would students choose to include and why? Using a common digital graphic organizer, a hierarchy of sections and links can be worked out and become the basis for a site map. Each of the sections shown on the map can then be done on a separate page. The word-processing program's typography and page layout functions, coupled with its ability to import, resize, and place a graphic, will allow for a satisfactory approximation of a real web site. A page of links to real online references to the author can be created after doing an online search and pasting the discovered "hits" into a fresh page.

Going just a step further, this mock site can be made real by creating hyperlinks within the document and, ultimately, after selecting Save As and choosing Web Page from the menu, opening the document within a web browser instead of on the computer desktop directly. Finally, students could send the site they have created to the author, care of the publisher, bringing the chain of reader, writer, web site consumer, and web site creator full circle. For more on creating real author web sites, see Chapter 6.

ADDITIONAL WEB SITES TO EXPLORE

K–3

Beatrix Potter

www.peterrabbit.com

www.beatrixpottersociety.org

Berenstain Bears

www.berenstainbears.com

Paul O. Zelinsky

www.paulozelinsky.com

William Joyce

www.williamjoyce.com

All Ages

Robert Sabuda

www.robertsabuda.com

Grades 4–8

Patricia Palocco

www.patriciapolacco.com

Brian Pinkney

www.brianpinkney.net

M. Sasek

www.miroslavsasek.com

Brian Selznick

www.theinventionofhugocabret.com

William Steig

www.williamsteig.com

Additional sources on other author/illustrators

Reading is Fundamental

www.rif.org

Kidsreads.com

www.kidsreads.com

Caldecott Medal Books

http://lib.mansfield.edu/caldecott.cfm

Coretta Scott King Book Awards

www.ala.org/ala/mgrps/rts/emiert/cskbookawards/

Ezra Jack Keats

www.ezra-jack-keats.org/

6

Creating Class Author Study Web Sites

Now that you and your students know about author web sites—how exciting, informative, and motivating they are—you can concretize and expand on what's been learned by beginning the process of creating your own site.

This activity is useful on a number of important levels. For one, reading, understanding, and appreciating literature is a rich experience, but really only one part of a natural continuum that logically leads readers to becoming writers as well. By creating your own author-focused web sites, your class will have a perfect way to integrate reading, writing, technology, and

CLASS ABC READS

Books We Love

Some good books we've been reading lately...

...and recommend you read, too!

| Figure 6.1 | Screenshot of a Class 123 Writes web site page, created and uploaded using Google Page Creator |

many others skills and bodies of knowledge into a seamless whole. All the elements for success are there, particularly high motivation through the authentic activity of creating and publishing a unique work that finds an appropriate audience, perhaps eliciting rounds of responses and feedback.

The overall experience is one that is firmly grounded in key curriculum areas, with a strong alignment to standards, but that is also open ended, allowing students to define what they want to know and do, develop their own challenges toward these ends, and explore. The work involves student research, creativity, and collaboration.

A Resource to Consult

No Strings Attached: Wireless Laptops in Education. This interesting professional development resource produced by the Florida Center for Instructional Technology at the University of South Florida's College of Education, offers many lesson plans that include video overviews. This one in particular relates to digital author study: http://etc.usf.edu/plans/lessons/lp/lp0124.htm.

The approaches and techniques all involve minimal purchase of technology resources, making extensive use of existing and free resources. Using them involves small learning curves, most of which can be tackled as self-learning/self-teaching through the abundance of online tutorials aimed at the technology novice.

In many cases, the components of a class author web site are actually discrete activities and products that may be done on their own with full value or that can be pulled into a whole that functions more as a repository of such products than as a product unto itself.

Equipment needs? Basically you'll need periodic access to half a dozen or more relatively up-to-date computers, at least one of which should have a relatively fast Internet connection. The software used in most cases amounts to little more than a word processor and a web browser.

THE TECHNOLOGY

Until relatively recently, having any web site for instructional purposes loomed as a mission nearly impossible to complete for the vast majority of teachers. The processes of web authoring, FTP (file transfer protocol) uploading of files, and server side site maintenance can seem hard to understand and thus precluded most teachers from establishing a web site as a resource. Even those who might have been able to master these skills had to contend with school district red tape and blatant distrust of the security and policy issues that accompany having a web presence. True, teachers in the know eventually were able to opt for cookie-cutter web site templates made available by a host of providers. But those offer very little in the way of customizing the look, feel, and navigational aspects of a site—the very things that make having a site to express a class's personality so appealing and special.

Now, however, with the advent of Web 2.0, also known as the *Read/Write Web*, it's all so much easier. Web 2.0 interactive resources make all web users potential web authors, a situation that invites teachers to do remarkable things with their students. These resources, such as blogs, wikis, podcasts, and interactive maps beckon to learning communities to make a splash in the biggest information pond ever created: the World Wide Web. And of course, once they become small fish in a really big pond, participants want to have something to say, and to say it effectively and eloquently so that their ripples reverberate and resonate with a world that is actually paying attention.

Platforms

Blogs

Blogs are the most well known, popular, and probably easiest to use of the Web 2.0 resources. Essentially, if you can create a word-processing document and, as a visitor/reader, can use web sites created by others, then you can create and maintain a blog (see Figure 6.2).

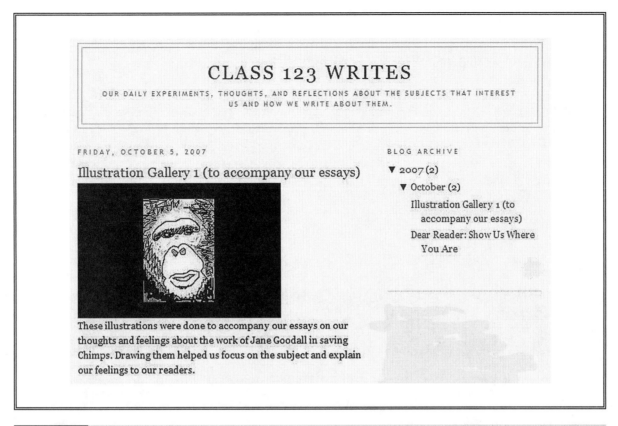

Figure 6.2   Screenshot of the Class 123 Writes blog, created using Blogger

And blogging platforms are very often free resources (e.g., Blogger; see www.google.com/ educators/blogger.html).

Blogs have their limitations, though. Generally, they lock the blogger in to a selection of templates that predetermine the kinds of features that can be incorporated and their layout on the page. The thought is that by offering a half dozen templates, a palette of common and effective blog formats is provided for the user to choose from and that should suffice for most users. Fortunately, while one really can't break with the template formats in a big way, they do allow for style elements (e.g., fonts, type colors) to be personalized. Many blogging platforms now allow for multimedia elements and live hyperlinks, to be embedded in the blog content, which makes them so very useful and requires that intermediate and advanced bloggers know how to acquire or produce digital photos, videos, and sound files.

One of the more advantageous features that blogs offer for the purpose of a class author site is the Comments feature. Since the aim, or one of them, in establishing the site is to have students communicate with an audience and learn from feedback, allowing readers to interact with the site by leaving comments becomes a very valuable aspect of the overall experience. As we have seen, many web sites of young people's favorite authors have a Guest Book feature. While there are numerous technology applications that can be used to create this, for those just beginning to dabble in technology use, the blog can perform this function very easily. Depending on the blogging platform, many allow for monitoring the comments before they are posted on the blog, a feature that will allay fears about inappropriate comments finding their way into the class's work.

TRY THIS WITH YOUR CLASS

Activity 6.1 Creating and Sharing a Class Book Blog

Grades 4–8

Blogs are a perfect format to keep a running, ongoing record of author study work done as part of an extended unit of study. It is easy for you or a class monitor to act as digital photographer of the class activities, taking a few shots each time the class works, which can be uploaded with the text of the day's activities. While blogs are organized for ongoing posts, one on top of the other, these can be confined to a single, long post yielding a web page that is vertically oriented instead of the typical horizontal layout.

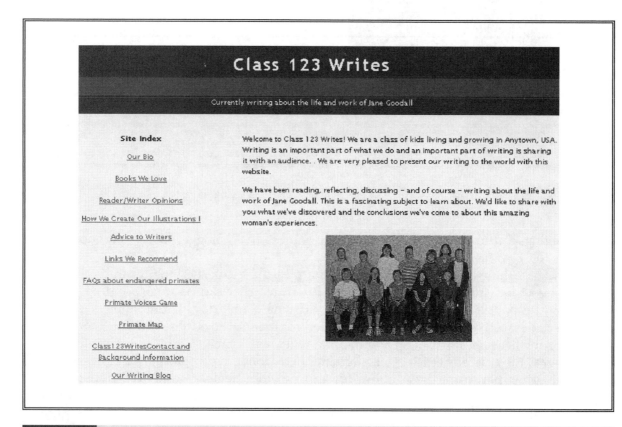

Figure 6.3 Screenshot of the Class 123 Writes home page, created and uploaded using Google Page Creator

There are other resources available that more closely resemble traditional web pages. These allow more elements to be displayed on a home page, with links to separate pages, all tied together through a hierarchical organizational scheme. The example given in this chapter was established using Google Page Creator (see Figure 6.3). Google Sites (http://sites.google.com), an improved resource, is now being offered instead of

Google Page Creator. In addition, the following resources are all free or low cost with a free trial period:

Scholastic's Class Homepage Builder: http://teacher.scholastic.com/homepagebuilder

TeacherWeb: http://teacherweb.com/tweb/NoticeNew.aspx

Homestead: www.homestead.com

SchoolNotes: www.schoolnotes.com

Wikis

A wiki is an online resource similar to a blog in many respects. Nothing special in the way of software or other resources or skills is required to establish and maintain a wiki. While a blog clearly separates the contribution of each poster, this is not the objective with a wiki. A wiki is conceived as an open group space, a place where all participants can come in and add to or change a group text (see Figure 6.4). Most teachers will likely opt for a more traditional web site or a blog, but for some special types of projects, the wiki may prove to be highly useful. Writing a collaborative piece of text with partner classes in remote locations, for instance, might be best facilitated with a wiki.

Wiki tools for educators need not be public and can easily be protected by using a password, making this a safe and secure resource. There are numerous wiki resources available (e.g., PBworks, http://pbworks.com) that offer a level of free service adequate for most classes' needs.

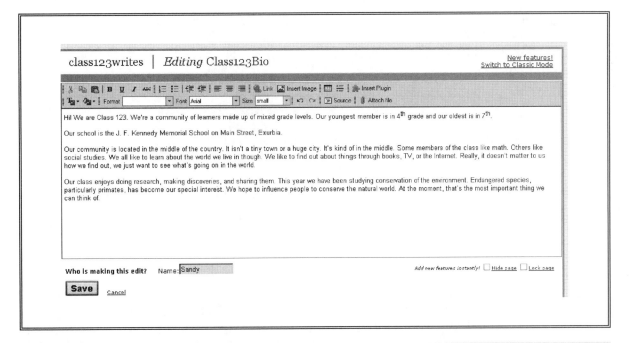

Figure 6.4 Screenshot of the Class 123 Writes wiki, created using PBwiki (now PBworks)

Composing, Uploading, and Hosting

While the new Web 2.0 publishing resources generally have removed the difficulties in putting things on the web, they do carry several limitations of their own. In addition to the less flexible formats available, they also allow for a lesser amount of data to be uploaded and housed on a subscriber's site or blog. This may be a prohibitive dimension for commercial organizations, but probably not for a class of students.

It is also the case that not every form of data may be uploaded, although this situation has gotten better recently. Blogger now allows uploading of photos (and other types of images saved in common graphics formats like JPG) as well as videos. Unfortunately, the types of file formats within these categories are limited. So with Blogger, for instance, JPG and GIF images may be uploaded, but not necessarily other graphics formats. The same is true for videos, in that not every format is compatible. Information is available on the web that will help you determine which formats can be used. And, of course, through a greater expenditure of time and effort, you can find information and resources to help you tackle the more difficult job of converting files from one format to another.

TRY THIS WITH YOUR CLASS

Activity 6.2 Creating and Uploading a Class PowerPoint Author Study Project

Grades 4–8

The organizational/navigational aspects of Microsoft PowerPoint make it a wonderful, easy-to-use program to support individual or collaborative projects.

1. Have students work as individuals or in groups.

2. Ask each student or student team to write a short piece based on research into a given author and paste this into a PowerPoint slide. Graphics downloaded from the web, original artwork scanned, or digital photos that students have taken can be easily imported into PowerPoint, resized, and positioned.

3. Have students turn their slides in to you so that you can merge them into a group presentation, giving it a cover or title slide to identify the students involved and introduce the theme.

4. Once the presentation is completed, upload it via a resource such as SlideShare (www.slideshare.net) or Scribd (www.scribd.com).

Many of the activities suggested throughout this book can be easily adapted and extended using this approach and type of resource.

The various blogging tools out there all have their own unique properties, capabilities, and characteristics. And generally, the free ones offer the user less. However, there is always more than one way to skin a cat. If you really want to put a PowerPoint file, for instance, on a blog and the blogging platform won't permit that format, then the next thing to do would be to search for an online resource that will accept this format. SlideShare (www.slideshare.net) is one that has been set up for just this purpose. Or you could create a slide show using a different resource. Picasa Web Albums (http://picasaweb.google.com), for instance, is one of numerous free photo-sharing sites out there that enables users to create slide shows.

Simple word-processed documents can be uploaded whole (that is, without altering their appearance from the way they look in hard copy) via document sharing web resources such as Scribd (www.scribd.com). Scribd offers a variety of views so that a document can be seen in its entirety, in close-up views of segments, or in thumbnails so that all pages of a multipage document can be seen simultaneously.

In the end, to get a media item into your web-published work, you will either upload it directly to the same server that hosts your web site or blog, or you will upload it to another server/resource and then insert the link from that into your published work. This may sound complicated, but after you have done it once or twice, it will seem like second nature and will become part of your intuitive thinking in planning future Web 2.0 work with students.

Some servers/resources offer yet another approach, embedding the interface directly into your work. This is currently popular in blogs and often you'll see the interface from YouTube or other video-sharing sites sitting square within a blog post. Accomplishing this is really as simple as copying the data from within a specified field on the video-sharing site and then pasting it into the blog post from within the HTML Edit function. Photo-sharing sites, including Picasa Web Albums, often offer this feature, too. Audio can be shared this way as well, but at this writing, doing so requires more effort and a steeper learning curve.

Sound is an element that can add greatly to students' online work. While many teachers who currently involve their students in making their own digital recordings call these *podcasts*, this is generally not quite the proper term for them. A podcast is a frequently updated audio file published online that is "pushed" to subscribers by Really Simple Syndication (RSS) technology (or that users can download from the podcast creator's web site). In most classroom situations, however, students will not be producing a show weekly or on some other set schedule; they may simply be producing a finite body of these pieces, which are not necessarily conceived as a series.

Regardless, the audio file must be uploaded to a server somewhere, as many of the Web 2.0 tools available will not accept them directly as uploads. You can search online for resources that will host these files (e.g., Ourmedia, http://ourmedia.org).

Rich Media Components for Your Class Author Site

Audio Recordings

As we've seen throughout this book, author sites are often enhanced with media items, particularly those that bring the real voice of the author to students. Audio posting/podcasting is part of a continuum of digital audio approaches and techniques that are now relatively simple and can be done by teachers and students.

Most laptops currently come with a built-in microphone. For teachers with older equipment or desktop computers without these, inexpensive microphones can be purchased from electronics stores for less than $10. The recording is done using audio software. Macs come with GarageBand already installed, and Windows users can download the free, easy-to-use Audacity (http://audacity.sourceforge.net).

Generally, the most practical approach to doing literature discussion podcasts is to set the classroom up theater style, with the performing literature group seated up front as in a panel discussion. The teacher can do the recording from a single laptop set up at the panel's table. The rest of the class appropriately functions as the audience for a live show, giving an appropriate role to everyone present. Groups can take turns at the head of the class, assuring that all students are actively involved.

The audio posting/podcasting process includes

- Creating the raw recording
- Editing and saving the recording in the proper file format (MP3 in the case of podcasts)
- Uploading the recording to a server somewhere that will accept it

Once recorded, the podcast can easily be linked to a class blog or web site or be burned to CDs for distribution to students, parents, and peers. If it is a true podcast, RSS technology will push it out from the podcast directory/host server. If the more applicable and practical *audio post* term applies, which may be one or several recordings, distributing the URL of the recording or embedding the URL as a link on a web site is the perfect approach. For a complete and easy-to-understand collection of information about podcast technology, curriculum suggestions, and classroom setup and management tips on classroom podcasting, see *Podcasting for Teachers* (King & Gura, 2009).

TRY THIS WITH YOUR CLASS

Activity 6.3 Researching Class Author Study Podcasts

Grades 4–8

Searching online using keywords like "student book talk podcast" will turn up numerous examples of schools and classes that record book talk–oriented activities digitally and then post them online for others to appreciate and learn from.

One such effort is R. A. Mitchell Elementary School Podcast Central (www1.gcs.k12.al.us/~podcast/mitchell.html), which contains many audio files. Another example is the web site of Bob Sprankle (www.bobsprankle.com/blog), a teacher from Wells, Maine, who records his third- and fourth-grade students' literature discussions and posts them as part of his popular, ongoing Room 208 podcast series.

By acquiring Skype (free Internet calling and chatting program; www.skype.com) and its Pamela recording application (low cost but not free; www.pamela.biz) interviews can be conducted over the Internet and recorded. The recordings done in Pamela (or similar software) can be edited and then used as part of an audio post or podcast. Remote interviewing may prove an invaluable platform for many literacy-rich activities that classes engage in as they produce content for their author sites.

Audio Plus Images

Audio items can be enhanced with accompanying graphics. It is becoming increasingly common for established software applications to be reissued with the capability to pair these two functions. The finished product will show the images coordinated with the sound on the screen of a computer, an iPod, or another MP3/MP4 player manufactured with this capability. In effect, this pairing produces something similar to a slide show that is accompanied by a soundtrack.

Photo Sharing

Free photo-sharing sites can give student photos (or drawings saved in similar file format, such as JPG) a web presence (see Figures 6.5 and 6.6). A link to students' online

Figure 6.5 Screenshot of the Class 123 Writes illustration gallery, created using Picasa Web Albums

Figure 6.6 Screenshot of a Class 123 Writes illustration in slide show mode, created using Picasa Web Albums

albums can be inserted into a blog post, enabling students to write and publish text to accompany their photos.

Digital Videos

The advent of YouTube and its many spinoffs makes it possible for video to be included in student author sites. Or videos may represent discrete activities and products on their own. As these projects are intended to be short, the digital video capacity of many reasonably priced digital still cameras, or even cell phones, may suffice to produce the raw footage. Editing can be accomplished with Windows Movie Maker (see Figure 6.7), which is included in the operating system of all Windows computers, or iMovie, a program that is often in the basic bundle of resources that comes with Macs.

TRY THIS WITH YOUR CLASS

Activity 6.4 Creating and Uploading a Book Trailer to YouTube

Grades 4–8

With the slide show capability of easy-to-use video-editing software, your class can create a book trailer for the works of a given author. The idea is to import still images in the chronological sequence in which they are to be shown in order to tell the story of the trailer. The amount of time that each is shown can be set in the software, which also supports adding text as well as recording and adding voice and music.

This project is heavy on reflection, research, and scripting/writing, with the technology dimension adding authenticity and motivation.

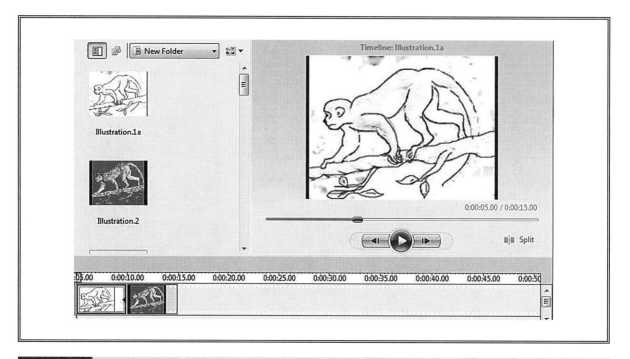

Figure 6.7 Screenshot from a presentation of the process of creating an illustration for the class web site using Windows Movie Maker

Web Site Authoring

You and your students can also create full-blown web sites without many of the format restrictions of blogs by using tools that obviate the need for special skills or software. The example given in this chapter (the Class 123 Writes web site) was created using Google Page Creator (see Figure 6.8). The limitation of this resource is that the site created had to conform to one of the templates provided. However, within the parameters established by a given template, a great deal can still be accomplished, much of it a near approximation of what an expensive, skilled, labor–intensive, professional web site would have. There is no web authoring or FTP uploading necessary, making this type of resource a model instant web site development tool. (Note that Google Page Creator has been replaced by Google Sites, which is similar although improved.) Take a look at the various components and their tech functions shown in the screenshots throughout this chapter to get an idea of how this resource can be used to create a class author site.

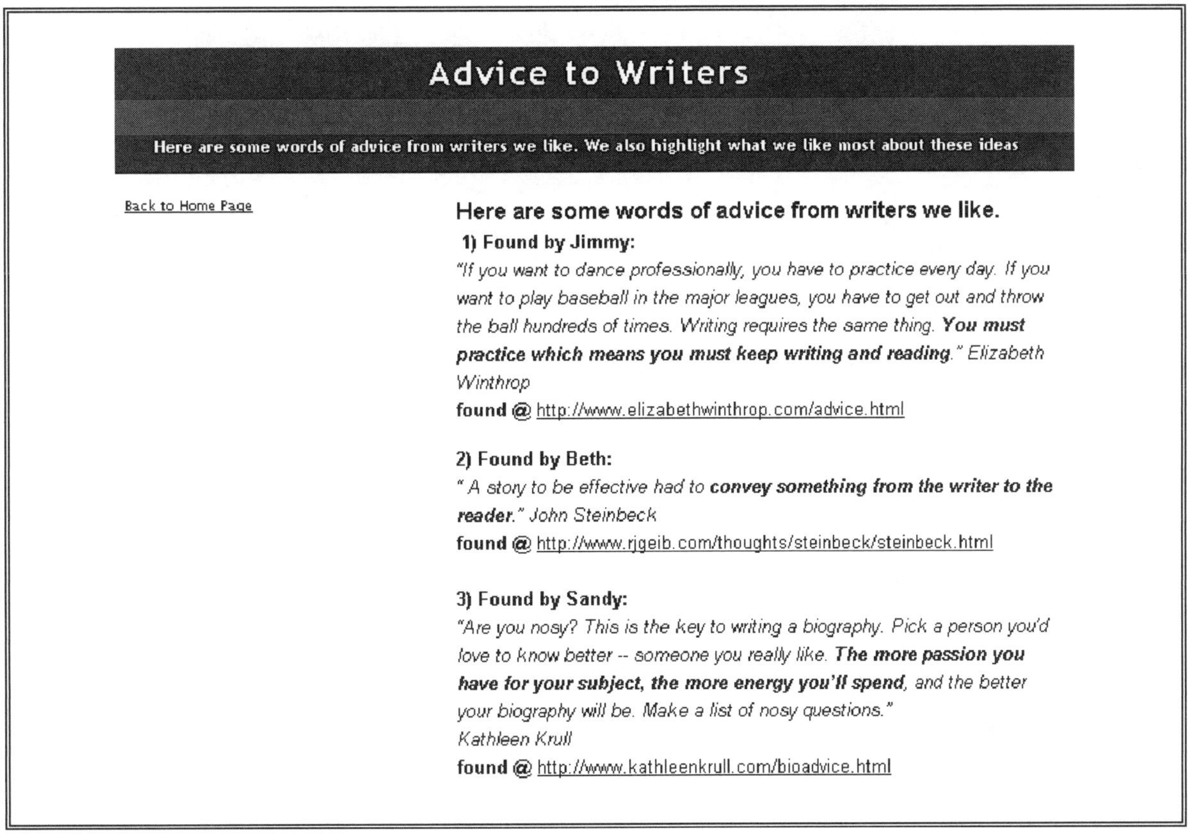

Figure 6.8 Screenshot of the Advice to Writers page of the Class 123 Writes web site, created and uploaded using Google Page Creator

Maps

Although not often considered publishing tools, the new generation of online maps can enhance student web sites as illustrations, often allowing a small amount of text to be included as well (see Figure 6.9). The digital map tool (e.g., Google Maps, http://maps.google.com; Frappr, www.frappr.com) is offered here as a resource to be used in the creation of class project sites and as an example of the type of Web 2.0 resource that is continually being developed for

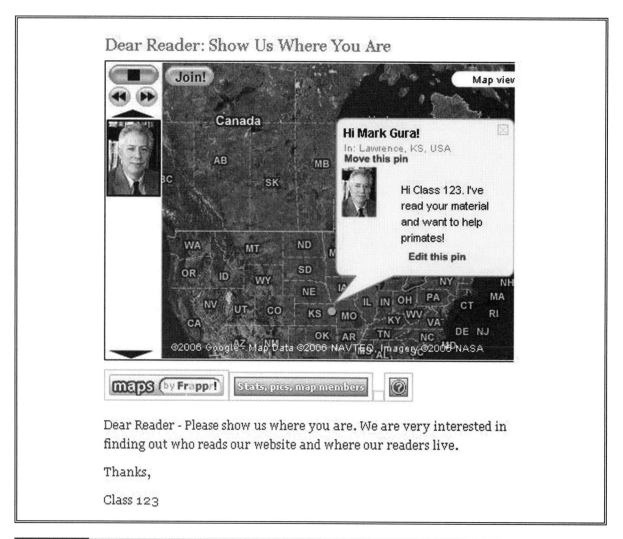

Dear Reader: Show Us Where You Are

Dear Reader - Please show us where you are. We are very interested in finding out who reads our website and where our readers live.

Thanks,

Class 123

Figure 6.9 Screenshot of the Class 123 Writes Frappr Map

use by creative people. A little web-based research will likely reveal others of interest. Searching for sites and blogs that discuss the latest developments and resources is an approach the will lead to an abundance of materials and information that can be used in the classroom.

Surveys

Free, easy-to-use online surveys can be used to take your class's author site efforts far beyond the classroom walls (SurveyMonkey, www.surveymonkey.com, is one example). Students can create an online survey form and disseminate it via the web or e-mail. Collecting original data sets on research projects distinguishes a class from simply reporting data collected by others and pulled from the web. This makes students active, focused researchers who can craft their own research projects. If the class's web site content is updated periodically, the use of surveys is a good way to add the element of interactivity between the class, the site, and its reading audience.

e-Books

Class web sites, especially those devoted to reflecting on and responding to the work of favorite authors, often include extensive amounts of text and student-created illustrations. For instance, as part of an ongoing semester-long unit of study, if each student in a class wrote one book review, and one research-based essay on a related topic, and created an illustration for each, anywhere from 60 to more than 100 pages of text are likely to be produced. These, of course, can sit on separate web pages and be linked to directories, allowing web site visitors to locate and access them for reading. However, while the experience of viewing and absorbing this material may be satisfying to visitors interested in reading or sampling a few, in other contexts it may be more satisfying if the material is collated and distributed in more traditional book format.

One of the beauties of writing and publishing in the Internet age is that the same material can be offered both ways, producing synergy. Organizing material originally conceived for a web site into a print offering is a worthwhile effort for a class, and one that will yield great insight into the nature of writing and publishing in our digital age. Once the organizing and design of the book is accomplished—something that can be greatly facilitated by the desktop publishing features of more sophisticated word-processing programs such as Microsoft Word—it is a simple matter to save the work as a visually faithful "locked" document using Adobe Acrobat, or another similar program, to produce a PDF file. Offering a full book of student work through the class web site is a great addition to whatever other material is presented there.

A simple search will turn up a wealth of online material on publishing e-books. Among many other resources are a free download from Adobe called *How to Create Adobe PDF eBooks* (www.adobe.com/epaper/tips/acr5ebook) and a host of suggestions about free software and resources from http://writers-publish.com.

e Mail Mr. Jones to order our Free eBook

www.JJ2@flatlands.net

Inspiration from Jane:
A collection of essays by Class 123 on the work of Jane Goodall.

Figure 6.10	Screenshot from the Class 123 Writes Contact Information page

Mixing and Matching Web 2.0 Elements

All of these tools and resources are designed to be used by people who engage in a short, simple self-teaching process—reading and following directions, doing a little experimentation, and building on similar items they've done before.

With a few baby steps under your belt, your imagination will be highly stimulated by the realization that the vast majority of Web 2.0 resources are compatible, making for a great many unusual combinations that organically satisfy the needs of class projects (see Figures 6.11 and 6.12). Once you are comfortable working in this new body of media, you will come to realize that the media extend literacy and vice versa, which leads to a wonderful new highly literate digital world to be created and explored.

What We Think and Feel
About this Subject (essays)

- **Inspiration from Jane**
  by Jimi

- **A Dffierent Kind of Hero**
   by Susan

- **Taking Care of Precious Things**
  by Marco

- **A Life Worth Living**
  by Phil

- **A Great Lesson to Learn in Africa by Channel**
  by Channel

Figure 6.11   Screenshot from the Reader/Writer Opinions page of the Class 123 Writes web site, created using Google Page Creator

Note: The links from this page go to full-page essays.

Inspiration from Jane

How this book has changed my understanding of things

Inspiration from Jane
by Jimi

Jane Goodall's lifework inspires me because she has made the world. The wonderful animals will all disappear from the people make it their business to watch out for them. There a

Figure 6.12   Screenshot from one of the Class 123 Writes student essay pages

THE CONTENT

Following the examples throughout this book of web sites established by many of the most read and beloved young people's authors, it is not difficult to map out great content for your own class's site. There is sufficient variety in the many different components of these sites to provide context, structure, modeling, and motivation for a good many student activities. The authors have developed these components to serve an authentic, organic need that has developed out of their genuine activities as writers and promoters of books. This includes a full cycle of activities: conceiving an idea, voicing and illustrating it, crafting and polishing it to conform to a format best suited for its intended audience, building and serving that audience by giving ancillary information—eliciting and responding to feedback—and reporting all of this publicly in an entertaining and informative manner on the web.

Types of Class-Created Author Sites

While any and all of this process can be appropriated outright, it is well worth the time and effort to reflect on how these elements emerge and function, and, in spirit as well as literally, to follow the example they set. In other words, the needs of each class are unique, and while it may elect to follow these examples, establishing new or altered approaches that serve its particular situation is very much in the spirit of what has gone before. The examples provided in this book are simply models, not hard and fast parameters. Their authors/developers tend to create new approaches as the need arises. And the new Web 2.0 reader/writer technology resources are simple and flexible enough to support that. The following are three kinds of sites that a class could create:

1. Student writers' site: Reading, writing, and publishing are a continuum of related activities that fuel one another. After students have enjoyed the excitement and enlightenment of the web sites of some of their favorite authors, their own writing can benefit immensely by creating an author site for themselves.

2. Fan site: Whether or not a favored author has a site that students can enjoy, they may wish to create their own site about that author and her work. Student responses to the target author's books, whether in the form of writing, artwork, digitally recorded audio of students discussing the books, or something else, can provide ample material for such a site.

3. Hybrid site: A class-created author site may be inspired by one or more favored authors and may include material created by students to support and capture their learning about that author and his work. It may also be a platform for publishing original student work inspired by and based on the work of the author.

The literacy activities involved in creating a class author web site may include the following approaches:

- *Research and reports based on that research:* This may include logging and presenting the sources and methods of doing the research; presenting the findings as traditional text essays or essays enhanced by a wide variety of digitally preserved, presented, or created illustrations; and developing simple media items to aid in the creation and shape the format of the report, such as slide shows, videos, or hyperlink-driven presentations (see Figure 6.13).

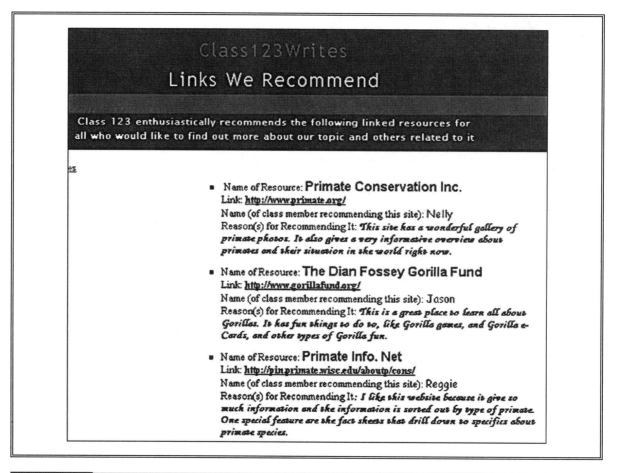

Figure 6.13   Screenshot of the Links We Recommend section of the Class 123 Writes web site

Note: The class uses this page to publish some of their research into information related to the work of their subject, Jane Goodall.

• *Reader reactions:* Essays or other forms of student writing (such as poems or dialogues) can capture the thoughts, feelings, and opinions of students in response to the work of the author who is the focus of their reading.

• *Reader reflections:* Reflections are similar to reactions, but with greater emphasis on analyzing the veracity, relevance, or impact of a studied author's work as well as the form and language in which it is presented.

• *Writing "inspired by" pieces:* Once students have read about a subject, and perhaps been involved in a series of group sharing activities to analyze and reflect on it, a logical next step is to write a personal work relating to it. This may include taking the same approach to subject selection as the studied author, writing another work on the same theme, or any of a host of extension projects such as mocking up additional material in the same voice or under the same name (fully acknowledged as such, though).

• *Procedural narratives:* Writing to describe in detail how things are done is often a required curriculum item that fits very well into the author site approach. In a number of the examples given in this book, author/illustrators give procedural narratives about how they

Figure 6.14 Screenshot from the Primate Voices Game page of the Class 123 Writes web site

do their illustrations or other aspects of preparing their books. Students can do the same. Preparing these for publication on a web site provides motivation, structure, and context.

Samples of Author Study Work Online

Author Study: Eric Carle: This elementary-level author study project was done by a class at Louise Sheffield Elementary School, in Jacksonville, Florida. This Microsoft PowerPoint product embraces many of the best features of author study.

http://mrscowan.com/EricCarleSlideShow.ppt

ThinkQuest Author Sites: This international competition showcases student-created information web sites. Its library of past submissions includes a number of very good author study projects done as web sites. Here are a few noteworthy examples:

www.thinkquest.org/library/cat_show.html?cat_id=135

http://library.thinkquest.org/J0111400/

(Continued)

(Continued)

http://library.thinkquest.org/5385/

http://library.thinkquest.org/J0110066/

http://library.thinkquest.org/TQ0013289/

Author Study Project: Seniors at Cary Academy, in Cary, North Carolina, produced this site as part of their class on The Great Books. The site describes the project and its objectives, explains which technology applications were employed, and provides a generous body of student work.

http://web1.caryacademy.org/facultywebs/carole_hamilton/author_stream_ALPHA.htm

Important Site Features

Following the lead of how the web sites of favorite authors have been constructed and organized, students should utilize a number of the following standard site features and sections in their own web efforts. Doing so can form the basis of highly worthwhile class activities.

- A home or landing page
- Biographical information (see Figure 6.15)
- Bibliography—an annotated listing of the class's writing projects (particularly those that have been published in some fashion and can be accessed by visitors to the site)
- Suggested links, with annotation explaining why they've been suggested and indicating what visitors will find there (see Figure 6.13)
- Reviews, testimonials, samples, and so on
- Interactive elements (galleries, videos, podcasts, GIF animations, PowerPoint presentations, and so on)
- Contact information
- Advertising and/or mock advertising (particularly to sell class-published books). Collections of student opinion and research can be produced as e-books and distributed through the class web site. For matters of practicality, offering them free is the simplest way to support this authentic learning activity without legal and school/district permission issues weighing down the fun.

ANNOUNCING YOUR SITE TO THE WORLD

Your Web Address

Before you do any work on your web-based publishing product, it is wise to consider the web address it will have. True, people will bookmark your item if it's something they like or have reason to return to time and again. But still, creating an address or URL that is easy to remember is a smart thing to do. People often find it easier to type in an address they remember instead of going through menus looking for bookmarks. It's also common for people to jot down in personal notebooks the addresses of resources recommended to them

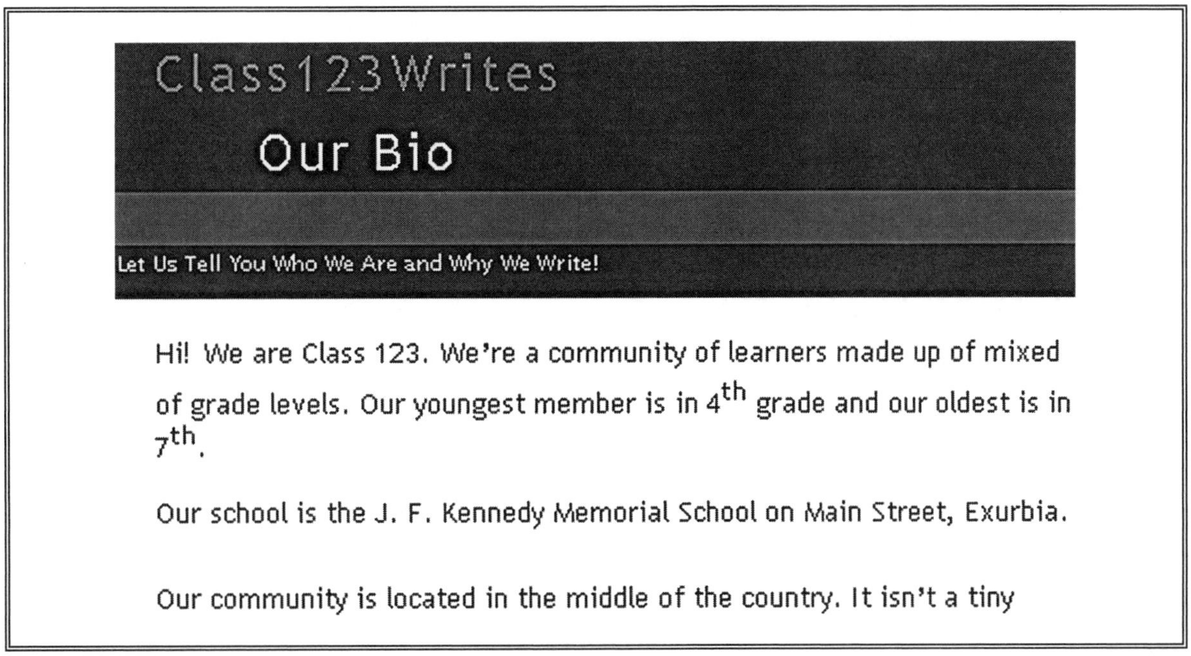

Figure 6.15 Screenshot from the Our Bio page of the Class 123 Writes web site

when they are not at their computers. Easy-to-remember addresses will help this process of word-of-mouth recommendation.

Also, when looking at long lists of bookmarks, it is easy to pass over something that doesn't jump out at you. If the name of your site is made a central part of its address, then this type of confusion is not likely to take place. A good example is http://class123writes.googlepages .com. At the heart of the address is the name, which is also a descriptor of what the item is and what function it performs for its authors. While you can't always control the entirety of an address from a free resource, keeping the core of it associated with you and your purpose will be helpful.

Hello!

Once you've created your site, you'll want to let people know about it. It is a simple matter to copy and paste the URL from a browser directly into an e-mail message and distribute it that way. An effective practice is to develop a short message, or signature, to put at the bottom of all e-mails you send out, announcing the web site and providing a live hyperlinked URL.

It may be effective to create a link from the school or district site to your class author site, steering general traffic to it and taking advantage of its function as a "best work" example of what students at your school can achieve. Similarly, a link from a parents or other community site can generate visitors.

Pinging

Once you've created your student-published resource, getting search engines to include it in their databases, and to position it favorably in the prioritization of search results, is an issue. Pinging services present your item and its ongoing updates to the search engines and aggregating services. It is simple to use these resources (e.g., Ping-O-Matic, http://pingomatic .com) through their simple online interfaces.

If you've created the web site as a blog, or have created a blog to accompany the site, you can establish an RSS feed for it to make certain that frequent updates are received and paid attention to by subscribers.

TRY THIS WITH YOUR CLASS

Activity 6.5 Online Class-to-Class Exchange Author Study Project

Grades 4–8

Using an online international student exchange resource (e.g., ePals, www.epals.com; iEARN, http:// iearn.org), your class can partner with foreign classes to collaborate on any of the student author study activities described throughout this book. Drawing on the digital product and dissemination ideas in this chapter, you can share the work with a very broad audience, lending greater authenticity to the activity and eliciting authentic feedback for students.

ISSUES TO CONSIDER

Legality

One of the most motivating approaches to fostering student writing involves its authentic publishing and presentation to real audiences. The techniques in this chapter suggest many ways to do that. However, because student work will be in the limelight, and because so much of what they write has to do with the work of others (either directly by writing about favorite authors or indirectly by reviewing the research items posted by others), intellectual property rights become an important consideration.

There are several dimensions to this issue. Presenting the concept of plagiarism is essential. However, it is important to probe a little deeper than that. Discussing the concept of intellectual property, its forms and limitations, is essential in having this subject make practical sense to students. Above all, intellectual property should be presented as something to be aware of and respected, but not an absolute stop to students' creative activities. The concept of proper citation should be presented as well as that of public domain and other approaches to properly and legally making reference to and appropriate use of the writing of others.

Privacy and Security

Blogs and wikis are generally considered public documents, that is, the motivation in creating them is most often to have them put before the largest number of eyes possible. However, depending on the specific instructional goal, this may not be the case for all student-created web-based items. It is possible to set the preferences so that the blogging platform does not automatically list the class's blog as one of the new submissions that the general public is invited to inspect. In a sense, the fact that a class's blog, web site, or wiki is online does not necessarily lead to anyone's awareness of its presence. These items are not necessarily submitted to search engines automatically.

Policy

In addition to the suggestions given in this chapter, teachers would be wise to check with local school and district regulations and policies concerning the publishing of student work. Furthermore, the district's Internet acceptable use policy should be consulted to verify that instructional practices are within the guidelines set for appropriate technology and Internet use.

While these projects involve a student presence on the web, in the interest of security they are conceived so that the identity of individual students need not be given. For example, Scholastic's Class Homepage Builder makes the following commitment to its teacher users: "Scholastic.com fully complies with the Children's Online Privacy Protection Act (C.O.P.P.A.) and helps you provide a secure, private Class Homepage for your classroom. Whenever you create a new item to post on your Class Homepage you will be reminded not to post any personally identifiable information about students, such as last names, school name, school location, e-mail addresses, home addresses."

Whenever direct contact with an anonymous or unknown audience may be involved, contact can be made through the teacher or another adult.

Appendix

Implementing Author Web Sites/Digital Author Study Activities

Curricular Connections, Pedagogy, and Standards

The instructional resources and approaches to their classroom implementation in this book represent revitalized takes on traditional materials and activities. These resources have been updated and translated to digital versions that take full advantage of the many communications innovations that have emerged as part of the Internet era. These curriculum items, and the methods and strategies for applying them, tap into technology to maximize student learning, resulting in enhanced experiences that address content as well as technology standards.

The author site approach is replete with opportunities for the use of higher-order critical thinking skills and student creativity. For example, students can be asked to develop a set of focus questions situated around the sections of a web site that the teacher has previewed. Students initially explore the site in search of information that provides answers to their own set of questions. They use the sharing component of the balanced literacy lesson to check and confirm the identification of responses to their questions.

As part of independent learning and reading activities, students can be given the option of designing their own webquests for author sites not covered in class. Then they can have their peers try out these webquests and share their responses.

The majority of projects, explorations, products, and portfolios associated with the author site approach engage students in collaborative problem construction, deconstruction, reconstruction, and reenvisioning of any author site investigated. These processes are initially followed using an author site student-evaluation rubric. As students become schooled in author site evaluation using this rubric, they have creative opportunities to modify the rubric to meet new criteria that they set. They can suggest new pages or new features for an author site, or they can prepare a home page and site map for a totally redesigned site. Students may also be allowed to demonstrate their collaborative and individual lateral problem-solving abilities and creativity by either designing from scratch an author site for an author who does not have an authorized site or developing a totally different site, perhaps for English Language Learners (ELLs), students with special needs, or peer student audiences.

Projects and experiences such as author impersonation or reenactments allow students to demonstrate their higher-order thinking and creativity capacities by reviewing and selecting relevant site data to use as part of their visual, spoken, and costumed performances and appearances as the author on their own school site.

In a similar manner, students are encouraged use their critical thinking skills and deconstructive problem-solving skills to integrate as many components as they can of an existing author site into an author expo, author celebration, or museum within school event.

Our author site approach is deliberately designed to be responsive to and reflective of content area standards developed by the following professional organizations:

- International Society for Technology in Education
- International Reading Association and National Council of Teachers of English
- National Council for the Social Studies
- National Research Council
- National Council of Teachers of Mathematics

Each of the selected authors, titles, and topics in our book explicitly addresses curricular themes and standards of these content areas. Throughout, the implementation of the author site approach addresses the National Education Technology Standards (NETS) of the International Society for Technology in Education (ISTE). In the following sections we focus on each of these sets of standards.

ALIGNMENT WITH TECHNOLOGY STANDARDS

The following table describes how author web sites and related online resources impact instruction directed at learning and achieving the NETS (ISTE, 2009). Since the author site approach focuses on use of the Internet and specifically on the design of author sites, it gives students in-depth experience with at least one key component of the Internet: the author site. Given this approach's extensive projects, reviews, and ratings of author sites and development of home pages and site maps for new author sites or site redesigns, students acquire a sound understanding of site construction, Internet research, launching of sites, site engines and indices, and key literature-themed resources.

NETS	Connection to Author Site Approach

1. Creativity and Innovation
 	
 Students demonstrate creative thinking, construct knowledge, and develop innovative products and process using technology. Students
 	
    a. apply existing knowledge to generate new ideas, products, or processes
 	
    b. create original works as a means of personal or group expression
 	
    c. use models and simulations to explore complex systems and issues
 	
    d. identify trends and forecast possibilities
	Through the study of author web sites and related resources, students benefit from the modeled creative activities of writers with whom they identify and whose work they have studied and been influenced by.
	
	    a. Following the process of extending the reach of a body of creative works through these web sites, students gain insight into the creative process and how it influences the outcome of ongoing work.
	
	    b. Seeking inspiration and direction from author sites, students are given a context replete with models and examples on which to base and channel their own creative needs and tastes.

NETS	Connection to Author Site Approach
	c. Media-rich and animated items on author sites, which enhance content that appears in their print books, make comprehension of the theme of their books more accessible by inviting understanding through alternate intelligences and learning styles. d. Readers are engaged in entire bodies of work and ongoing creative initiatives as opposed to single works. They are empowered to draw inferences from the works of single authors and compare these with inferences of numerous writers addressing the same, similar, and related themes.
2. Communication and Collaboration Students use digital media and environments to communicate and work collaboratively, including at a distance, to support individual learning and contribute to the learning of others. Students a. interact, collaborate, and publish with peers, experts, or others employing a variety of media and formats b. communicate information and ideas effectively to multiple audiences using a variety of media and formats c. develop cultural understanding of global awareness by engaging with learners of other cultures d. contribute to project teams to produce original works or solve problems	Author sites are interactive, inviting students to use technology to join an extended community of students, register for newsletters and ongoing news and updates of author activities, sign and leave messages in guest books, and ask questions and advice of professional writers. a. Author sites often motivate the establishment of forums and discussion groups among interested readers as well as communication with one another directly through the sites' interactive features. b. Author sites model how mass communication is achieved through both print books and online formats. c. Author sites provide a common body of interest and information as well as a conduit for information. They have broad appeal across geographic and cultural borders. d. Author sites are digital learning resources that lend themselves in many ways to collaborative and small-group work among students.
3. Research and Information Fluency Students apply digital tools to gathering, evaluating, and using information. Students: a. plan strategies to guide inquiry b. locate, organize, analyze, evaluate, synthesize, and ethically use information from a variety of sources and media	Author sites are sources of information and clearinghouses for additional sources of information on an author's interests, themes, and works. a. As a discrete form, they challenge students with information, categories, and media, and require strategized efforts to absorb their content.

(Continued)

(Continued)

NETS	Connection to Author Site Approach
c. evaluate and select information sources and digital tools based on the appropriateness to specific tasks d. process data and report results	b. Author sites serve specific functions and require students to analyze how well they perform these, the approaches taken, and their relative merits and characteristics as an emerging form of communication. c. Author sites model how a variety of formats may be used to expand on and communicate a central theme or body of work. d. Author sites establish a vivid format on which students may base their own reporting of information and ideas.

4. Critical Thinking, Problem Solving, and Decision Making
 	
Students use critical thinking skills to plan and conduct research, manage projects, solve problems, and make informed decisions using appropriate digital tools and resources. Students
 	
  a. identify and define authentic problems and significant questions for investigation
 	
  b. plan and manage activities to develop a solution or complete a project
 	
  c. collect and analyze data to identify solutions and/or make informed decisions
 	
  d. use multiple processes and diverse perspectives to explore alternative solutions
	Author sites provide appropriate and relevant material as the basis for challenging student activities
	
	a–d. Author sites are repositories of material on real-world problems and investigations. They identify, explain, and model these problems and investigations. They illustrate solutions and the approaches and methodologies employed to arrive at them for a variety of purposes, including theme selection, project structure, processing of research findings, and expression of results.

5. Digital Citizenship
 	
Students understand human, cultural, and societal issues related to technology and practice legal and ethical behavior. Students:
 	
  a. advocate and practice safe, legal, and responsible use of information and technology
 	
  b. exhibit a positive attitude toward using technology that supports collaboration, learning, and productivity
 	
  c. demonstrate personal responsibility for lifelong learning
	Author sites offer content based on human, cultural, and societal issues that serve as themes for popular works of fiction and nonfiction.
	
	a. Author sites highlight specific issues (e.g., racism, censorship, character issues, environmental concerns), engaging students in reflective activities about them.
	
	b. Author sites illustrate and model how communications technology resources can positively impact such issues.
	
	c. Author sites encourage students to identify and take a personal position on a variety of issues and begin to engage in constructive actions and proactive citizenship.

NETS	Connection to Author Site Approach
d. exhibit leadership for digital citizenship	d. Author sites model and demonstrate the basis for small- and whole-group activities based on important issues in which leadership qualities and understandings may develop appropriately.
6. Technology Operations and Concepts Students demonstrate sound understanding of technology concepts, systems, and operations. Students a. understand and use technology systems b. select and use applications effectively and productively c. troubleshoot systems and applications d. transfer current knowledge to learning of new technologies	Author sites embrace a full range of communications and media technologies. a. Author sites provide an engaging structured (virtual) environment in which the systems behind the sites can be observed and analyzed. b. Author sites model highly appropriate communications projects to inspire and guide similar student work. c. Author sites involve a wide variety of user and authoring skills when made part of student activities. d. Author sites are part of a continuum of technologies, all of which build on current versions as they evolve.

ALIGNMENT WITH ENGLISH LANGUAGE ARTS STANDARDS

As educators begin to tap the resources of the growing number of author sites, they can note that classroom use of these sites and assigning them for independent research and study projects addresses the purposes and goals of the *Standards for the English Language Arts* (International Reading Association & National Council of Teachers of English, 1996).

Author sites provide multiple opportunities for students to develop the language skills necessary for proactive citizenship and global social success. Interacting with and engaging in online activities offered on author sites helps students make productive use of their literacy abilities. The standards that the author site approach are aligned with are discussed below.

1. *Students read a wide range of print and nonprint texts.* Use of the author site as an extensive text for author study, in addition to the printed texts of the author's work, offers students opportunities to read a wide range of nonprint texts.

3. *Students apply a wide range of strategies to comprehend, interpret, evaluate, and appreciate texts.* The author site approach offers a broad spectrum of ideas for minilessons and ways for small groups and individual learners to explore the author's site and themes, including the following: author impersonations for author celebrations; museum-within-school author exhibits; exchanges of ideas, reviews, reactions, and responses with learners in other locations; collaboration with other readers and with the author on author-developed writing prompts; rubric-driven student review of author sites; design of an author site for an author who does not have one; and an invitation to develop a list of additional links that are pertinent to the existing author site.

4. *Students adjust their use of spoken, written, and visual language (e.g., conventions, style, vocabulary) to communicate effectively with a variety of audiences and for different purposes.* The author site approach empowers students to run their own classroom/school-based site expo; impersonate an author or key characters from the author's work using authentic biographic, speech, and other character details from the web site; develop pop-up or life-sized character figures; design an environment for their classroom or hall display that reflects the visual themes, ideas, or illustrations of the author/artist; and develop their own position papers and readers theater versions of texts or prompts found on the author site.

5. *Students employ a wide range of strategies as they write and use different writing process elements to communicate with different audiences and for a variety of purposes.* Among the wide range of strategies and writing process elements, the author site approach includes opportunities for extensive prewriting and pre-web-site-design outlining; authentic research within a particular genre or theme; revision based on site visitor or author response; publishing to the author site guest book, message board, or site newsletter; and doing readings of the author's texts in the style of site audio clips of the author's personal text readings.

7. *Students conduct research on issues and interests by generating ideas and questions and by posing problems.* In the author site approach, students can conduct research on and pose questions about many author-centered themes and issues such as the environment and how students/adults can work toward saving the planet (www.tabarron.com), racism and the extent to which racial attitudes as surveyed really reflect our multicultural reality in the United States (www.faithringgold.com), and censorship and free speech (www.judyblume.com).

8. *Students use a variety of technological and informational resources (e.g., libraries, databases, computer networks, video) to gather and synthesize information and to create and communicate knowledge.* The author site approach, with its accompanying mix of audio and video clips, sound effects, and databases as well as its use of web design analysis/evaluation opportunities, taps into the potential to realize this standard. Students can design a new web site feature for an existing author site and/or a home page and site map for an author who does not have a site. They can also use Dreamweaver and Flash software programs for their own author-inspired web designs. Furthermore, they explore key children's literature resources and site engines as part of this approach.

9. *Students develop an understanding of and respect for diversity in language use, patterns, and dialects across cultures, ethnic groups, geographic regions, and social roles.* Many author sites are deliberately focused on the issue of diversity in language (e.g., Carmen Lomas Garza, www.carmenlomasgarza.com; Sandra Cisneros, www.sandracisneros.com; Gary Soto, www.garysoto.com; Julia Alvarez, www.juliaalvarez.com) and dialects (e.g., Faith Ringgold, www.faithringgold.com; Tomie dePaola, www.tomie.com). Through thoughtful study of these web resources and the authentic voices of their authors, students gain immediate exposure to and interaction with a vast spectrum of cultural and regional understandings.

10. *Students whose first language is not English make use of their first language to develop competency in the English language arts and to develop understanding of content across the curriculum.* The author study approach provides a particularly effective pathway for ELLs to achieve equity in balanced literacy instruction and engagement. Through using carefully selected author sites that include languages and cultures other than and in addition to American English (e.g., Luis Rodriguez Jr., www.luisjrodriguez.com; Gary Soto, www.garysoto.com; Sandra Cisneros, www.sandracisneros.com; Lesléa Newman, www.lesleakids.com; Carmen Lomas Garza, www.carmenlomasgarza.com), ELLs can gain immediate access to

culturally and linguistically affirming texts. Reading and writing activities incorporate languages other than English and include mouse-drawn, click-and-drag games (e.g., on the site of Sandra Cisneros) and opportunities to share perspectives in their native language and to upload a drawing or audio reflection. The multimedia components of many author sites make balanced literacy come alive for even the most recent newcomers to the United States. For students whose families do not model storytelling literacy, as well as for the class as a whole, author sites can provide read-alouds.

11. *Students participate as knowledgeable, reflective, creative, and critical members of a variety of literacy communities.* This is the essence of author site study. Student visitors gain knowledge about the author's life, times, purposes, achievements, and perspectives. Part becoming more knowledgeable in this way involves exploring reviews, the bio, resources, photos, comments of other readers and peers, and links related to the author. For teachers and older students (Grades 4 and up), there are specific lesson plans, resources, articles, and other activities to review. Visitors of all ages can become part of the online communities nurtured by author sites by subscribing to the free newsletters and participating in discussions, chats, forums, online collaborative projects, writer's prompts, and other exchanges on these sites.

12. *Students use spoken, written, and visual language to accomplish their own purposes (e.g., for learning, enjoyment, persuasion, and the exchange of information).* Opportunities for students who use author sites to publish their reviews and commentary on the author's works, themes, multimedia offerings, and so on in guest book entries or other sections of the sites ensure that students can authentically accomplish their purpose. This authentic purpose is often validated for students by a specific response either directly from the author or from the webmaster or overseer of the site. In addition, the nature of author sites is conducive to distanced, diverse, multisector reader conversations. In this way, the sites serve as an online book circle for reader participation. Students can also upload and share their illustrations in the style of the author/illustrator's art or to show how they would visually represent an author's theme. The author site approach includes specific and deliberate visual arts and web design activities to tap real-life skills in service of creating or reconfiguring author sites that effectively accomplish the author's mission.

ALIGNMENT WITH SOCIAL STUDIES STANDARDS

The author site approach aligns with the 10 thematic strands of the social studies standards of the National Council for the Social Studies (NCSS, 1994). It should be noted that a large number of authors, even those whose works are fictional, incorporate grade-, content-, and age-appropriate social studies themes within their literature and in their web site activities, student-centered opportunities, and teacher options. The NCSS strands and their alignment with the author site approach are detailed below.

Culture

Social studies programs should include experiences that provide for the study of culture and cultural diversity . . . In a democratic and multicultural society, students need to understand multiple perspectives that derive from different cultural vantage points. This understanding will allow them to relate to people in our nation and throughout the world . . . The study of culture prepares students to ask and answer questions such as: What are the common characteristics of different cultures? How do belief systems, such as religion or political ideals of the culture, influence the other parts of the culture? How does the culture change to accommodate different ideas and beliefs?

Through their experiences with multicultural literature and the broad spectrum of international and multiethnic authors whose web sites are included in the author site approach, students and teachers can literally hear, experience, and explore various cultural perspectives. Many author sites focus on celebrating particular ethnic groups, backgrounds, storytelling traditions, and historical events through the filter of a specific cultural perspective.

The author site approach serves as a kinesthetic, visual, auditory, interactive, and intrapersonal entry point for students whose learning styles are not specifically linguistic and text based so that they can experience and explore particular authors' perspectives. Even for students whose learning style and intelligence strengths are text based, the capacity to click on supportive visual, auditory, map, graphic, and interactive survey options/button enables them to access culture in a dynamic and ever-changing fashion. Also, the multiple language options afforded by the author sites offer immediate access to newcomers and ELLs.

The vibrancy, dynamism, and interactivity of various sites by an increasing large number of multicultural authors affirm the diverse identities of students and their families and provide pertinent geographic, historic, anthropological, and sociological data. Many authors included in this approach openly address the key cultural concepts of adaptation, assimilation, acculturation, and diffusion in a way that makes these abstract concepts very real in photographic, auditory, musical, and interactive modes.

Time, Continuity, and Change

Social studies programs should include experiences that provide for the study of the ways human beings view themselves in and over time. . . . Knowing how to read and reconstruct the past allows one to develop a historical perspective and to answer questions such as: Who am I? What happened in the past? How am I connected to those in the past?

The author site approach is ideally suited to making the past come alive beyond even photographic historical nonfiction or vivid memoir. For example, many sites include interactive games and video clips that allow learners to experience time, continuity, and change in a dynamic multisensory fashion. Indeed, for many ELLs or learners who have cognitive disorders, author sites and other multimedia resources offer optimal vehicles for experiencing these key concepts.

This NCSS strand recommends that learners "in early grades gain experience with sequencing to establish a sense of change and time." Author sites can literally provide graphic meaning for this concept via presentations of historical or plot sequences and timelines with clickable animated, audio, or video icons.

People, Places, and Environments

Social studies programs should include experiences that provide for the study of people, places, and environments. Technological advances connect students at all levels to the world beyond their personal locations. . . . In the early grades, young learners draw upon immediate personal experiences as a basis for exploring geographic concepts. . . . During the middle school years, students relate their personal experiences to happenings in other environmental contexts.

Many authors who have established and authorized web sites strongly support protection of the environment and share information about particular places and landforms. In particular, T. A. Barron's site (www.tabarron.com) is rich with a distinctive mapping section that lends geographic reality to his fictional and mythical adventure series. Jean Craighead George's site (www.jeancraigheadgeorge.com) has multimedia, audio clips, and maps that showcase how author sites can serve as a concrete online teaching and learning tool for this key strand.

Of course, these very mapping, geography, and place themes are also a key part of document-based questions on standardized social studies and other content exams. By providing interactive and game formats, the author site approach furthers test-sophistication skills and high academic achievement. Since maps are accessible for ELLs and visual/kinesthetic learners, the author site approach provides these students with access to this strand.

Individual Development and Identity

Social studies programs should include experiences that provide for the study of individual development and identity. . . . In the early grades . . . [by] observing brothers, sisters, and older adults, looking at family photo albums, remembering past achievements and projecting oneself into the future . . . young learners develop their personal identities in the context of families, peers, schools, and communities. Central to this development are the exploration, identification, and analysis of how individuals relate to others.

Through the use of its various features, an author site, whether it is authorized or unauthorized, fosters a strong sense of the author's individual development and identity. Activities in almost all author studies focus on the author's biography and how it influences the author's writings and themes. All author sites include bios, which often include photo galleries, videos, and author memoirs as well as commentary by colleagues and family members.

These web resources are all about the authorship of one's personal identity as an individual, which then resonates in one's writings. Thus, visiting author sites directly connects students with key components and venues for studying individual development and identity.

Individuals, Groups, and Institutions

Social studies programs should include experiences that provide for the study of interactions among individuals, groups, and institutions. Institutions such as schools, churches, families, government agencies, and the courts all play an integral role in our lives. . . . The study of individuals, groups, and institutions draw[s] upon sociology, anthropology, and other disciplines.

The author site approach focuses on many authors whose works are motivated by various institutions such as schools, churches, families, and the courts. Many of their historical fiction and biographical and memoir documentation deal with institutional change from a historic or personal/familial/ethnic perspective. In addition, many authors use the multimedia outreach and cyber community town meeting potential of their web sites to advocate for what they view as ways to work through institutional change for common good.

Science, Technology, and Society

Social studies programs should include experiences that provide for the study of relationships among science, technology, and society. . . . [T]echnology brings with it many questions: Is new technology always better than that which it will replace? What can we learn from the past about how new technologies result in broader social change, some of which is unanticipated? . . . How can we manage technology so that the greatest number of people benefit from it? How can we preserve our fundamental values and beliefs in a world that is rapidly becoming one technology-linked village?

To some extent, the whole concept of the author site approach is inherently a response to and a test case for this strand. The very concept that an author's work and his or her life concerns can be researched online in a matter of seconds, as opposed to going to a public library to research articles, biographies, photos, and secondary books about the author, highlights the choices and opportunities afforded by technology versus the traditional print texts. Use of author sites by younger and middle school students facilitates their acquisition of the basic search and evaluative tools of technology-use skills, which should monumentally increase their present and future research efforts.

Global Connections

Social studies programs should include experiences that provide for the study of global connections and interdependence. Analysis of tensions between national interests and global priorities contributes to the development of possible solutions to persistent and emerging global issues in many fields. . . . Analyzing patterns and relationships within and among world cultures, such as . . . age-old ethnic enmities, political and military alliances, and others, helps learners carefully examine policy alternatives.

The author site approach offers a perfect technology entry point to documenting, demystifying, and engaging students in making meaning and connecting in a global fashion. For example, a visitor Jane Goodall's site (www.janegoodall.org) can make instant and meaningful informational, firsthand, and responsive connections with its mission of global connectivity and responsive actions on behalf of people, animals, and the environment. Through the Action Alerts page (in the News section), students can send, via snail mail or e-mail, "polite letters" to various individuals who have been involved in recent advertisements or programs using chimpanzees for a cheap laugh while modeling animal cruelty. The web site even provides templates for students to use. Every student can immediately be part of making a difference for chimps in the media and in society.

Related to another aspect of this NCSS strand is the web site of the Anne Frank Center (www.annefrank.com). Students can view an online scrapbook and perhaps use the images to make emotional and cognitive global connections between racism in different parts of the globe at different times in recent history. They can also learn about the Spirit of Anne Frank

Awards, the recipients of which receive scholarships and stipends for having "demonstrated outstanding commitments to take a stand against discrimination of all kinds." Encourage students to spread the word and celebrate those who embody this spirit by nominating a peer or teacher for this award.

Civic Ideals and Practices

Social studies programs should include experiences that provide for the study of the ideals, principles, and practices of citizenship in a democratic republic. . . . Learners confront such questions as: What is civic participation and how can I be involved? . . . What is the balance between rights and responsibilities? . . . How can I make a positive difference?

As previously discussed, the author site approach fosters student and teacher participation as readers and as citizens by providing immediate access to the authors themselves. For example, by exploring Lesléa Newman's site (www.lesleakids.com), readers can be encouraged to volunteer as Big Brothers or Big Sisters. The site provides links to student-centered civic participation programs such as America Writes for Kids. Many other authors use their sites as a citizenship activism platform, encouraging initial letter writing, e-mailing, and use of newspapers as the first defense against abridgement of civic ideals and practices.

ALIGNMENT WITH SCIENCE STANDARDS

The *National Science Education Standards* (National Research Council, 1996) "present a vision of a scientifically literate populace" (p. 2) The emphasis in the overview of these standards is excellence and equity through a rich array of learning materials within the basic premise of science as an active learning process with both hands-on and "minds-on" experiences. As part of the inquiry-driven style of science explorations, students are inculcated with the use of describing objects, asking questions, constructing hypotheses, formulating meaning, testing their own reasoning against current scientific knowledge, and sharing their responses with others.

The author site approach, with its capacity to offer a rich array of multimedia, video, audio, and interactive resources pertinent to a given science topic, can support this vision of a scientifically literate populace. Certainly, students who independently tour and explore an author's web site must do so in a "minds-on" fashion as they share perspectives, communicate their own explanations and hypotheses with peers and adults, and become part of an online science literacy community. Many of the activities, prompts, and constructive actions to save our planet and support all living things engage students in using their communication skills.

Among the Science Content Standards, the following resonate with and are enhanced through use of topic- and theme-appropriate author site study:

- Science as Inquiry
- Science and Technology
- Science in Personal and Social Perspectives
- History and Nature of Science

Focusing especially on Science as Inquiry, the standards envision "inquiry into authentic questions generated from student experiences [as] the central strategy for teaching science"

(p. 31). The author site web designs, with their frequently asked questions (FAQs), guest books, links, chat rooms, and forums, are poised to be responsive to authentic student questions. Author study involving the works of Jane Goodall (www.janegoodall.org), Mem Fox (www.memfox.net), Seymour Simon (www.seymoursimon.com), Gail Gibbons (www.gail gibbons.com), Doreen Cronin (www.doreencronin.com), and Jean Craighead George (www.jeancraigheadgeorge.com) would be replete with author site or related web resource opportunities. Many of the steps and stages of formulating questions, collecting data, and presenting findings to others for their constructive criticism are enabled and expanded through the use of the distanced and broad audience of author site visitors, including adult readers, content experts, teachers, librarians, peer students, and the author or webmaster of the author's site. Since one of the desired teacher methods for fostering student inquiry in learning is to "orchestrate discourse among students about scientific ideas" (p. 32), how better to do so than visiting an author site to discuss the scientific principles and implications of that author's work or using the links on the site to identify other online exchange and collaborative science communication and constructive action possibilities?

In terms of student inquiry–driven methodologies, the standards suggest that teachers "challenge students to accept and share responsibility for their own learning" (p. 32). The author site approach enables students to accept and share this responsibility through numerous collaborative and individual student action projects, including redesign or design of peer age-appropriate author web sites and development of new features and activities for existing author sites, which can include student representations, models, experiments, generalizations, and chat discussion boards or interactive science content games and quizzes. Use of the sites as a platform for sharing this learning with the site audience affords immediate feedback for students and literal publication of their efforts for their teachers, peers, and family to view.

ALIGNMENT WITH MATHEMATICS STANDARDS

The author site approach has been successfully used by K–8 teachers to integrate author study, balanced literacy, and mathematical process and content standards acquisition, per the National Council of Teachers of Mathematics (NCTM, 2000) *Principles and Standards for School Mathematics*.

Principles

Four of the six NCTM principles can be addressed through the author study approach.

- *Equity: Excellence in mathematics education requires equity—high expectations and strong support for all students.* Often because of non-English-language backgrounds; special needs accommodation requirements; or spatial, kinesthetic, intrapersonal, auditory, and other learning styles beyond the standard mathematics textbook linguistic approach, students are denied access and equity to excellence in mathematics education. Yet through the use of both print and online sources (e.g., Aunty Math, www.auntymath.com; Greg Tang, www.gregtang.com; Math Solutions, www.math solutions.com), students are afforded online, musical, spatial, interactive access to excellence in mathematics education.
- *Learning: Students must learn mathematics with understanding, actively building new knowledge from experience and previous knowledge.* The emphasis on actively building

new knowledge is precisely what the author sites for mathematics topics in children's literature are all about. Sites such as Greg Tang's offer games and insights into students preparing their own puzzles, problem constructs, and word problems using fables, patterned rhyme, and sing-song stories. Aunty Math's site involves students in building the new language of lateral solutions to online challenges, which are rooted in authentic real-life situations and other experiential contexts that require using past mathematics knowledge to build new knowledge.

- *Assessment: Assessment should support the learning of important mathematics and furnish useful information to both teachers and students.* Through the use of interactive author site games, activities, explorations with online scoring, commentary, and progressions from one level of mathematics knowledge and processes expertise to the next, students can set goals, assume responsibility for their own learning, and become more independent learners.

- *Technology: Technology is essential in teaching and learning mathematics; it influences the mathematics that is taught and enhances students' learning.* The use of technology as students access author sites and use their mathematics knowledge and skills to solve problems provides them with many authentic online opportunities for decision making, reflection, and reasoning. Author sites also offer useful mechanisms such as guest books, scoring systems, challenge feedback, and customized problem construct responses that validate and enhance the authenticity of students' efforts. The author site approach integrates the versatility and power of technology in service of mathematics content and mathematics communications fluency.

Standards

Content Standards

Using the author site approach with authors who purposely create both fiction and nonfiction books in line with targeted mathematics elementary programs addresses the following content standards:

- *Number and Operations:* This standard focuses on young children developing an understanding of the structure of the base-ten system and elementary and middle school students performing computations in different ways. Using mathematics-centered author sites enables students to make communication-centered connections and use graphics and animations to authenticate number and operations. In addition, various sites, such as Aunty Math with its numerous challenges, allow students to realize the standard's goal of explaining their method, understanding that many methods exist, and seeing the usefulness of methods that are efficient, accurate, and general.

- *Algebra:* This content standard conceptualizes algebra as a style of mathematical thinking for formalizing patterns, functions, and generalizations. The standard advocates introducing algebraic mathematical thinking, reflecting, and reasoning among even young children as they investigate patterns and relations among sets of numbers. How better to concretize children's mastery, increasing fluency and comfortableness with algebraic thought, than through visual, spatial, and interactive problem solving connected to the web sites of Aunty Math, Dr. Math (http://math forum.org/dr.math), and Greg Tang.

- *Geometry:* In geometry, students at all grade levels analyze shapes and characteristics of shapes and make mathematical arguments about geometric relations. This content standard advocates the use of visualization, spatial reasoning, and geometrical modeling to solve problems. It explicitly suggests that "geometry is a natural area of mathematics for development of students' reasoning and justification skills." Sites such as Dr. Math and Aunty Math include numerous references to spatial reasoning and require students, in responding to FAQs or in answering challenges, to use reasoning and justification skills. Therefore, these and other content-related author sites (e.g., Greg Tang, www.gregtang.com; Math Solutions, www.mathsolutions.com; Mem Fox, www.memfox .net) provide wonderful literacy-linked online opportunities to develop and enhance these necessary skills. Even through reading the summaries of published fiction and online problems featuring Aunty Math and her nephews and niece, students are able to experience the real world and fictive world connections between abstract content standards and everyday life.

- *Measurement:* As this standard emphasizes, measurement is integral to many aspects of the K–8 curriculum. By using specific author web sites tied to books on measurement, students can not only demonstrate online their ability to understand various aspects of measurement, they can also explore and justify making decisions about units and scales that are appropriate for problem situations using storytelling and procedural account narrative skills.

Process Standards

Even more than the content standards, the process standards are inherently aligned with and enhanced by targeted use of the author site approach.

- *Problem Solving:* This standard emphasizes the building of new mathematical knowledge from decontextualized skills, mathematics-driven problems, and those embedded in the context of a fiction or nonfiction work. Students can just as easily demonstrate this standard by adding on adventures for children's mathematics literature schema (e.g., for *The Greedy Triangle* or *The King's Commissioners* in the Marilyn Burns Brainy Book Day Series) and sharing these via the author's web site. As students work—not only to write these added scenarios for mathematics-centered literature formats, but also to critique their ongoing plot lines with peers and teachers—they are also adapting via the writing process a variety of appropriate problem-solving strategies. Inherent within the process of developing these scenarios or even responding to prompts on author sites is reflection on the process of mathematical problem solving.
- *Reasoning and Proof:* This standard is all about having students not only recognize reasoning and proof as fundamental aspects of mathematics, but also make and investigate mathematical conjectures, design and evaluate mathematical proofs, and select various types of reasoning. As students visit author sites and read various mathematics-centered trade books (by, e.g., Mitsumaso Anno, Greg Tang, Marilyn Burns, Harriet Ziefert, Donald Crews, John Scieszka, Jim Haskins), they are actively engaged in solving online word problems and responding to fictive and real-world mathematics concerns through using language to detail their reasoning, proof, and conjecture process.
- *Communication:* Using author sites and assigning/accessing trade books that deal with mathematics principles and process standards furthers students' consolidating of their mathematical thinking through communication. When they go online and become part of a mathematics author's community of readers, problem solvers, mathematical strategists, and mathematics detectives, they have to communicate their mathematical thinking clearly and coherently to distanced authors as well as peer and adult visitors.

- *Connections:* Almost every mathematics-centered author makes connections between mathematics principles, concepts, and process standards, and concretizes these connections through a fiction or nonfiction narrative structure. For example, for K–2 students, *The Silly Story of Goldie Locks and the Three Squares,* by Grace Maccarone, makes connections between classic fairy tales, geometric shapes, and the principle that the shortest distance between two points is a straight line. This funny and engaging story (plus the shape hunt, shape picture, and problem explanation prompts, all of which can be found on the Math Solutions site) demonstrate how mathematical ideas interconnect. Conducting a mathematics author expo or having students enact a "personal" visit with a mathematics author would be a wonderful way to make the Connections standard come alive in a classroom setting.
- *Representation:* Author sites, particularly those of Aunty Math, Greg Tang, and other mathematics-oriented authors, are virtual representations that organize, record, and communicate mathematical ideas. As students explore a site like Aunty Math's to respond to online challenges related to selecting, applying, and translating among mathematical representations to solve problems, they experience, navigate, and utilize these representations toward targeted solutions.

In addition to authors whose total trade book content is focused on mathematical standards and processes, many key author sites of major trade book writers and illustrators include works and activities that model, interpret, and draw on physical, social, and mathematical phenomena (e.g., Seussville, www.seussville.com; Shel Silverstein, www.shelsilverstein.com).

Resources

Although this book is designed to immediately enable its readers to apply the classroom field-tested activities and approaches featured here, these best practices are informed by the work of a broad spectrum of theorists and researchers. The following list can serve as an introduction to a select number of these individuals.

Atwell, N. (1998). *In the middle: New understanding about reading, writing, and learning* (2nd ed.). Portsmouth, NH: Heinemann.

Atwell, N. (2002). *Lessons that change writers.* Portsmouth, NH: Heinemann.

Atwell, N. (2005). *Naming the world: A year of poems and lessons.* Portsmouth, NH: Heinemann.

Atwell, N. (2007). *The reading zone: How to help kids become skilled, passionate, habitual, critical readers.* New York: Scholastic.

Atwell, N. (2008). *Day to day assessment in the reading workshop: Making instructional decisions in grades 3–6.* New York: Scholastic.

Calkins, L. M. (1994). *The art of teaching writing.* Portsmouth, NH: Heinemann.

Calkins, L. M. (2000). *The art of teaching reading.* Boston: Allyn & Bacon.

Cambourne, B. (1995). Toward an educationally relevant theory of literacy learning: Twenty years of inquiry. *Reading Teacher, 49*(3), 182–198.

Cooper, J. D., & Kiger, N. D. (2008). *Literacy: Helping students construct meaning.* New York: Houghton Mifflin.

Daniels, H. (2001). *Literature circles: Voice and choice in book clubs and reading groups.* York, ME: Stenhouse.

Fletcher, R., & Potalupi, J. (2002). *Craft lessons: Teaching writing K–8.* York, ME: Stenhouse.

Fountas, I. C., & Pinnell, G. S. (2009). *The Fountas and Pinnell leveled book list K–8+.* Portsmouth, NH: Heinemann.

Fox, M. (2001). *Reading magic: Why reading aloud to our children will change their lives forever.* New York: Harvest Books.

Freeman, Y. S., & Freeman, D. E. (1998). *ESL/EFL teaching: Principles for success.* Portsmouth, NH: Heinemann.

Gardner, H. (2004). *The unschooled mind: How children think and how schools should teach.* New York: Basic Books.

Gardner, H. (2006). *Multiple intelligences: New horizons.* New York: Basic Books.

Keene, E., & Zimmerman, S. (1997). *Mosaic of thought: Teaching comprehension in reader's workshop.* Portsmouth, NH: Heinemann.

Lankshear, C., & Knoebel, M. (Eds.). (2006). *New literacies: Changing knowledge and classroom learning.* New York: Peter Lang.

Miller, D. (2009). *The book whisperer: Awakening the inner reader in every child.* San Francisco: Jossey-Bass.

Pinnell, G. S., & Fountas, I. C. (2007). *The continuum of literacy learning grades 3–8: A guide to teaching.* Portsmouth, NH: Heinemann.

Rosenblatt, L. (1969). Towards a transactional theory of reading. *Journal of Reading Behavior, 1*(1), 31–51.

Routman, R. (1996). *Literacy at the crossroads: Crucial talk about reading, writing, and other teaching dilemmas.* Portsmouth, NH: Heinemann.

Routman, R. (2005). *Writing essentials: Raising expectations and results while simplifying teaching.* Portsmouth, NH: Heinemann.

Schwartz, S. (2008). *A quick guide to making your teaching stick.* Portsmouth, NH: Heinemann.

Zemelman, S., Daniels, H., & Hyde, A. (2005). *Best practice: Today's standards for teaching and learning in America's schools* (3rd ed.). York, ME: Stenhouse.

References

Blume, J. (Ed.). (2001). *Places I never meant to be: Original stories by censored writers.* New York: Simon & Schuster.

International Reading Association & National Council of Teachers of English. (1996). *Standards for the English language arts.* Newark, DE, and Urbana, IL: Authors.

International Society for Technology in Education. (2009). *National educational technology standards for administrators.* Washington, DC: Author.

King, K. P., & Gura, M. (2009). *Podcasting for teachers: Using a new technology to revolutionize teaching and learning* (Rev. 2nd ed.). Charlotte, NC: Information Age.

National Council for the Social Studies. (1994). *Expectations of excellence: Curriculum standards for social studies.* Silver Spring, MD: Author.

National Council of Teachers of Mathematics. (2000). *Principles and standards for school mathematics.* Reston, VA: Author.

National Research Council. (1996). *National science education standards.* Washington, DC: National Academy of Science.

Strickland, D. S. (1997). Balanced literacy: Teaching the skills and thrills of reading. *Instructor, 106*(8), 42–45.

Index

CORWIN

A SAGE Company

The Corwin logo—a raven striding across an open book—represents the union of courage and learning. Corwin is committed to improving education for all learners by publishing books and other professional development resources for those serving the field of PreK–12 education. By providing practical, hands-on materials, Corwin continues to carry out the promise of its motto: **"Helping Educators Do Their Work Better."**